CANINE CROSS TRAINING

Building Balance, Strength and Endurance in Your Dog

Sasha Foster, MSPT, CCRT

Wenatchee, Washington U.S.A.

Canine Cross training
Building Balance, Strength and Endurance in Your Dog
Sasha Foster, MSPT, CCRT

Dogwise Publishing
A Division of Direct Book Service, Inc.
403 South Mission Street, Wenatchee, Washington 98801
1-509-663-9115, 1-800-776-2665
www.dogwisepublishing.com / info@dogwisepublishing.com

Photos: Sasha Foster
Graphic Design: Lindsay Peternell

Limits of Liability and Disclaimer of Warranty:
The author and publisher shall not be liable in the event of incidental or consequential damages in connection with, or arising out of, the furnishing, performance, or use of the instructions and suggestions contained in this book.

Library of Congress Cataloging-in-Publication Data

ISBN: 978-1-61781-113-5

Printed in the U.S.A.

More praise for *Canine Cross Training*

This is a comprehensive, detailed source for targeted canine exercises. It's thoughtfully conceived and well-written—an essential go-to guide.

M. Christine Zink DVM, PhD, DipACVP, Professor and Director Department of Molecular and Comparative Pathobiology, Johns Hopkins University School of Medicine, author of *The Agility Advantage* and *Peak Performance.*

To Quin

Black fur shining, running in the bending green reeds beside cool high mountain streams, you taught me to love with dedication so deep it rooted me to the world. May you always have smooth wet stones on which to rest your belly and fields of fresh bright snow.

I miss you, Boo.

TABLE OF CONTENTS

... Ellie Bennet, for preparing the manuscript. Co ...

ACKNOWLEDGMENTS

This book would not have been possible without the tremendous dedication and hard work of the following people: Ashley Foster, who works effortlessly by my side reminding me to see the world through the eyes of the dogs; Pam Foster and Jim Simos, my parents, for guiding me with your experience; Dr. Jana Dean, Dr. Greg Burns, Dr. Rainey Corbyn and the staff at South Mesa Veterinary Hospital and Come, Play, Stay in Fort Collins, Colorado, for your continued dedication to impeccable veterinary medicine, animal rehabilitation, and boarding and daycare services; all *Canine Fitness Zone*™ clients, for your wonderful feedback helping me better understand how to help you provide research-based care for your dogs; Sarah Stremming, for editing again and again and sharing ideas that made this book better; Craig Miles and staff, for your tremendous dedication to my business; Steve Carroll, for teaching me the language of numbers; to the Larimer County Small Business Administration including Jim McWilliams, for turning a book into a business; Monica Wilson, for being Quin and Mimzy's friend and companion while I'm off sharing ideas with the world; Yvonne Hanning, mother of May, for editing and superb feedback on the original manuscript; Ashley Eike, for citation editing; Ellie Bennett, for prepping the manuscript; Corrine Glulick, for creating forms in the eleventh hour; and all the people who believe that dogs deserve the highest quality research-based care available. Your efforts are greatly appreciated.

INTRODUCTION

The brain of a physical therapist is an interesting place. Trained to see with our hands and calculate with our eyes, our observation skills become honed to the point where we can't turn them off. The dog pacing in the park has back pain, that agility dog has limited hip range of motion and this old dog has a sore right knee. Of course, unless asked, we generally keep these constantly trolling thoughts to ourselves. But the point is that our senses are trained to see movement and our brains are trained to do something about it. Furthermore, when we make recommendations, be it a conditioning program for a healthy dog or a physical therapy treatment for an injured dog, we should always have a good physiological reason for choosing each little thing that we do. Making decisions based on the body's natural processes is part of the art of physical therapy. Healing and wellness occur because we understand how to facilitate the body's inherent wisdom. Knowing how best to use the body's natural processes to promote wellness and healing is the basis of canine cross training.

When I decided to start *Canine Fitness Zone*™ , the goal I set was to build a cross training program based on well-founded physiological principles and primary research. The result was a program I call the *4-Tiered Canine Athletic Conditioning Program* which forms the basis of this book. Not only did I want to improve the physical performance of dogs through cross training, I also wanted to use only positive, reward-based training methods that would teach not just exercises for dogs, but would modify their bodies so what they learned in our dog gym would carry over into life. I quickly learned that creating exercises was fairly easy. Creating exercises that humans could teach dogs to do with good form following the neurological principle of "motor learning" was another thing all together. You'll read all about motor learning in Chapter Two.

The process of canine exercise development is an intellectual challenge that requires humor and patience. In the beginning, as I did my research and developed new exercises, I would get all excited about it and run to the dog trainers, Ashley and Sarah, at South Mesa Vet Hospital in Fort Collins, Colorado where my original physical therapy clinic is located. I'd say "Hi, how do I get a dog to side step onto a six inch box with his back legs without touching him in any way?" They'd look at me and shake their heads as I pulled the box out and hoped someone would let me borrow their dog. Together we would sit on the floor and work out not just how the exercise should be done from a physical therapy perspective, but how the exercise should be done from the dog's perspective. We challenged each other to think better, harder and outside the box. In the process we helped Sarah develop a new method for agility running contacts. We also threw down a few challenges, for example, "First one to teach her dog to climb up a wall backwards wins!" (Check out the *Canine Fitness Zone* channel on YouTube to see which dog won.) In time we became very good at putting our brains together—a physical therapist/certified pet dog trainer brain fusion that created foundation exercises and behaviors to safely and effectively execute the movements. The program presented to you here is what was created in this process. It is founded on conditioning research and created with a dog's physical, mental and emotional terrain in mind.

The research used to develop this program spans many years and multiple species. Opossums were kind enough to teach us how quadruped muscles store energy for movement. Rats and cats taught us most of what we know about nerves. Humans showed us how muscles respond to strength training. And dogs, bless their hearts, taught us about the canine cardiac response to exercise. Together this wonderful body of research was a good starting point for designing our canine cross training program.

But please understand, just as the *4-Tiered Canine Athletic Conditioning Program* frequently undergoes modifications, the information presented in this book will need to change as well. As the body of canine-specific research grows in the emerging field of animal rehabilitation, we expect to learn things we simply do not know now. Please forgive the mistakes I don't know I'm making today. Rest assured I will continue to update this work to bring your dogs the highest quality, research-based, physical-therapy-brained conditioning programs currently available.

Who needs this book

My primary goal in writing this book is two-fold. One is to provide a manual on cross training for Certified Canine Rehabilitation Therapists (CCRT), physical therapists and veterinarians who have completed continued education for canine rehabilitation. The other is to address the needs of dog enthusiasts who have their dogs compete in a growing number of canine sport activities, many of which place significant physical demands on their dogs. While the number of CCRTs is growing nationwide, not everyone interested in cross training will have personal access to their expertise. While I recommend that a cross training program should be initiated under the supervision of a CCRT, a well informed dog enthusiast can utilize the knowledge in this book to help their dogs succeed in the cross training exercises.

Safety first and two quick notes

Conditioning programs should not be initiated lightly. A dog's body must be healthy enough to handle the stresses of exercise. Safe implementation of balance exercises requires healthy ears, eyes and nerves. Initiation of strength exercises demands healthy joints, ligaments and muscles. Endurance exercises need a healthy heart and lungs. By virtue of a dog's dedication to survival, they will do their best to hide injuries making it impossible to always see these problems with your eyes. A thorough veterinary assessment is *always required* to determine baseline health and clear a dog before beginning a cross training and/or conditioning program. Optimally, a Certified Canine Rehabilitation Therapist should then be consulted if you have access to one to complete a conditioning evaluation to assess joint and joint capsule integrity, muscle extensibility, posture/muscle balance, strength baseline and baseline endurance. If not, follow the guidelines carefully in this book. A health assessment will provide important pieces of information to help determine which exercises are most advantageous for the dog and which exercises should not be initiated, particularly if a dog has a history of movement issues such as knocking bars in agility.

If in the course of a veterinary assessment a health issue is found, it will not necessarily prevent your dog from participating in a conditioning program. Your vet may clear your dog to participate with certain restrictions due to minor health issues. In this case, however, I strongly urge you to seek the services of a CCRT who can design and develop a plan that takes your dog's physical limitations into account. In that way you can be assured that your dog is able to meet the conditioning goals you have set without over-stressing a weak, injured or impaired body system.

Please don't risk your dog's health. Safety first.

A couple additional notes. Some of you may have read the book that I co-authored with my sister Ashley Foster titled *The Healthy Way to Stretch Your Dog - A Physical Therapy Approach*. While it is not necessary that you read that book prior to this one, cross training and stretching go hand in hand in many instances. I refer to *Stretch Your Dog* in instances where the stretch routines included in it complement the recommendations in this book. Key terms throughout this book are shown in bold to alert you of their importance.

Equipment

To safely and accurately complete many of the exercises, fitness equipment is needed. (All equipment can be purchased at www. caninefitnesszone.com.) This equipment should be stored and brought out only for cross training exercises. When exercise equipment is involved, your dog should be already trained to respond to your verbal/hand cues or commands. Your dog must be able to wait for your signal before he interacts with any equipment. Improper use of equipment can place a dog at risk of injury.

The in-home dog gym: Yoga mat or non-skid surface; clicker and high value treats; white tape for markers; high motivation toy for brain breaks; balance disc, (<45# = small, >45# = large); pair of balance stones; elbow-height box (yoga block for mini and toys); ½ elbow-height box (yoga block for mini and toys); balance peanut (upside-down balance stone for mini and toys); wobble board; and balance board.

CHAPTER 1

Conditioning Components and Principles

A canine cross training program blends balance, strength, endurance and flexibility exercises into a fitness program that can be tailored to specific conditioning goals, modified for different activities, and adapted throughout the life of a dog. It is the fastest and most effective way to achieve complete health at any age or stage of life. Rooted in basic research, the program contains the four **conditioning components**—balance, strength, endurance and flexibility (please read *The Healthy Way to Stretch Your Dog: A Physical Therapy Approach* for stretching instructions and routines to build flexibility)—and the exercises are executed following **conditioning principles** including exercise frequency, intensity and duration. When an exercise program includes all four conditioning components and each is completed following proper conditioning principles, all body systems are trained to work at optimal levels. This means more robust body systems are prevented from compensating for weaker systems, a scenario that sets the body up for predisposition to injury. When exercises are completed with this level of care and consideration, they are safe, effective and meet each dog's individual fitness needs. Young dogs will improve body awareness, canine athletes will increase competitiveness and old dogs will maintain mobility. No matter what the age or activity level, a cross training program harmonizes the body bringing out a dog's natural grace and vitality.

Conditioning tailored to your dog

This cross training program is tailored to the needs of your dog. Before any exercise program is undertaken, tests should be conducted to measure the dog's balance (core stabilization), strength and endurance. The results of these tests are employed to measure your dog's current fitness and are used to determine which of the four levels of exercise regimes is appropriate for your dog at the beginning of his cross training program. For example, a core stabilization test (see Chapter 3) is used to determine which exercise level is appropriate to help improve your dog's balance. As you read through the book, keep in mind this process of testing first and then selecting the appropriate exercise level.

Conditioning components

The conditioning components—balance, strength, endurance and flexibility—are the foundation of a cross training program. Exercises that improve the four components increase the fitness level of a particular body system. Balance optimizes nerve reactions so the body responds to the environment with lightening speed. Strength improves muscles forces, storing power that moves the body. Endurance increases heart and lung efficiency, supplying energy that can be used for short sprints or long runs. And stretching after exercise maintains elasticity of muscle fibers preparing them for the next bout of exercise (Barroso et. al., 2011). When a conditioning program includes all of these exercise components, it becomes a cross training program. The body systems become inextricably linked so performance outcomes improve, the risk of injury decreases and, most importantly, overall quality of life improves.

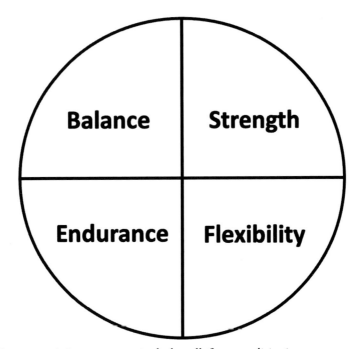

A cross training program includes all four conditioning components: balance, strength, endurance and flexibility.

Conditioning principles

Conditioning principles are the research-based rules of exercise execution. They are the safest, most effective way to execute a cross training program (Wilmore and Costill, 2004). Founded in physiology, they define the exercises, when they should be completed and for what length of time. If exercises are completed following these principles, the likelihood of meeting the conditioning goal is very high. If the rules are followed randomly, the goal will be elusive.

Principle 1: Overload

The principle of **overload** states that the body will only increase balance, strength, endurance and flexibility if the body is asked to do more than it is doing now. In other words, overload, an increase in exercise intensity, is required to stimulate the body to increase its fitness level. When initiating a cross training program, it is important to determine the correct amount of overload. Too little will not create a training effect to improve a dog's performance, too much will cause compensatory movements which can be detrimental to the dog.

Overload is determined with balance, strength and endurance fitness tests. Stretching does not require a test. Stretching intensity is always, "Until you feel slight resistance, then hold for fifteen to thirty seconds." Please see *The Healthy Way to Stretch Your Dog* for further details. The outcome of the tests defines which intensity level of exercises should be initiated (Level One, Two, Three or Four). Once the level for each conditioning component is determined, exercises can be handpicked or an activity specific cross training program can be chosen from Chapter 6. The exercises are then completed following very specific guidelines for each conditioning component. These include:

- **Frequency.** How many exercise sessions should be completed per week.
- **Intensity.** How many repetitions of each exercise should be completed per session.
- **Duration.** The length of each exercise to be completed per session.

Principle 2: Cellular adaptation

When exercises with proper overload are initiated, the cells in the body respond by changing internally to meet the increased demands required of the exercises (Coffey and Hawley, 2007). For each of the conditioning components, the cells adapt following a series of physiological events that are accomplished within a specific time frame that cannot be modified by any external factor. For example, when strength exercises are initiated twice a week with 48 hours between sessions, the muscle cells begin changing to increase strength. The process of increasing strength to meet the demands of the new exercises takes about twelve weeks. At this three month mark, for a given exercise regimen, strength improvements will plateau. This time frame is due to the process of **cellular adaptation**, physiological processes that cannot be shortened no matter which exercises are completed or how often.

Principle 3: Progression

When the body has completed the process of cellular adaptation, conditioning improvements will plateau because the body is acclimated to the increased demand placed on it by the exercises. If further improvements in conditioning are required, the exercise intensity level must be increased, or progressed. When the dog begins the new exercises, the physiological time clock of cellular adaptation begins again. **Progression** of a cross training program should continue for each conditioning component until the cross training goal has been met. When the goal has been met, the exercises should continue or the body will **reverse the training effect**. See Principle 6, Use and Disuse below.

Principle 4: Training specificity

This principle states the cells in the body respond to exercises in very specific ways. Balance exercises augment balance. Strength exercises build strength. Endurance exercises improve endurance. Stretching exercises increase flexibility. **Training specificity** guides a cross training program by ensuring the exercises match the conditioning goals. For example, when training an agility dog to be more dexterous on the course, the employment of balance exercises, specifically whole-body awareness exercises, will help meet this goal. Strength, endurance and flexibility exercises will not improve dexterity on the course but they are important for different reasons; strength increases drive off the start line, endurance will increase course speed and flexibility can prepare the muscles for the next bout of exercise.

Principle 5: Breed differences

The body contains different **muscle fiber types**, the proportion of each of these being largely a function of genetics. Dogs who were bred for long distance running, such as Alaskan Huskies, are naturally better suited to endurance activities. If you want an Alaskan Husky to weight pull, a conditioning program can be created to increase his strength. But with all the conditioning in the world, the Husky would probably not beat the small but powerful Staffordshire Bull Terrier who has a genetic predisposition for strength.

Principle 6: Use and disuse

A reversal of the training effect—a decrease in strength, endurance, balance and flexibility—can occur from **disuse** with only a four week break from training (Mujika and Padilla, 2000). This means that if conditioning stops for just a few weeks of rest, you may need to extend the length of the conditioning program with the current exercises to ensure the body has completed the cycle of cellular adaptation. Many months of rest require re-starting a conditioning program at the beginning. Balance, strength and endurance fitness testing should be completed again to ensure the correct intensity levels of exercises are chosen so the exercise intensity is not too difficult.

Building a fitness program that includes exercises from all four conditioning components and executing those exercises following these conditioning principles does something very powerful for our dogs. It provides them with the same high quality conditioning programs that many people benefit from. By providing dogs with this quality of care, their lives can change for the better. Young dogs don't have to tolerate teasing for poor rear limb awareness. Athletes can far exceed current world records. And old dogs can have high quality of life for many more years. All of this is possible because of the fusion of all body systems through exercises that support the health, vitality and joy that is cross training.

CHAPTER 2

Motor Learning

On the surface, asking a dog to complete exercises appears simple. In truth, teaching the body sound and efficient patterns of movement is a very complicated process termed **motor learning** (Simon and Bjork, 2001). In general terms, motor learning is teaching the body new patterns of movement that carry over into daily, performance and sporting activities. This is achieved by asking the dog to complete exercises on his own with good posture and control. When exercises are completed in this manner, the body learns new patterns of movement in response to two neurological processes. **Cognitive learning** is the ability of the brain to receive novel input and make an action decision based on that information (Foerder, et. al., 2011). **Neural plasticity** is the ability of the body to create new nerve pathways to execute the action decision (Warraich and Kleim, 2010). When these two processes become integrated, as occurs when quality exercises are completed over a number of months, the body becomes very adept at learning new patterns of movement and then carrying these movements into a multitude of different situations and environments. This is the goal of cross training: taking the improvements in balance, strength and endurance and making them automatically accessible during daily activities, sporting activities and performance events to optimize the body's output while decreasing the probability of sustaining injuries.

The process of motor learning

New motor patterns occur because the body functions as an integrated whole. When a dog completes an exercise, nerves in the muscles send signals to the brain describing body position. These signals are combined with other signals including visual (from the eyes) and vestibular (from the ears) to form an action decision (Lisberger, et. al., 1987). This process of sending and receiving signals from muscles to brain and back to the muscles again **encodes**, or maps, novel movement patterns into the nervous system. If exercises are completed with good posture and excellent control, the body will encode a high quality pattern and this, in time, will carry over into other activities. When poor quality movements are encoded into the nervous system, this low quality movement is encoded and will carry over into other activities. Whether high quality or low quality, once neural encoding has occurred it takes a tremendous amount of consistent effort to overcome the pattern (Kostrubiec, et. al., 2011). Therefore it is worth taking the time to learn how to teach exercises correctly from the start.

Completing exercises with good posture and control improves the quality of neural encoding.

Training method for quality neural encoding

To ensure quality neural encoding, proper exercise training methods are needed. The recommended training method is termed **shaping by successive approximation** (Garrett, 2005). Shaping provides the dog the opportunity to complete the exercises without physical intervention from the handler. With this training method, the dog's voluntary action is paired with a positive stimulus, a reward, which encourages the dog to repeat a behavior. When this pairing of events is recurring, for example stepping on the disc with a reward for the behavior, the depth of neural encoding deepens which increases the probability that the movement will carry over into other activities.

If this training method is not used, for example the handler places the dog on the equipment rather rewarding the dog to learn to do it himself, neural encoding will still occur but it will include the handler's touch. This decreases the probability of the movement pattern being accessible outside of the training session since independent movement patterns have not been encoded. When the dog is asked to repeat the behavior on a new piece of equipment, for example to place the back paws on a peanut instead of a box (as will be required to increase the intensity of core stability), the behavior won't be recalled because it doesn't exist. The dog will expect assistance because that is what was learned during exercises. Most importantly, when the dog is in a performance event and the front limbs slip on wet grass, the core stabilizers—the muscles strengthened with the exercises—won't have the benefit of independent neural encoding for contraction of these spine-stabilizing muscles.

The only way to ensure that the balance, strength and endurance achieved in a cross training program carry over into activities outside of the dog gym is to have the dog complete the exercises independently with good form and control. Shaping is the best way to ensure that quality neural encoding occurs. Teaching a dog to step on to the equipment using shaping may take longer, perhaps a few additional training sessions, than simply placing the dog on the equipment. But in the long run, the dog who is trained this way will become very fast at learning new exercises, and because of neural encoding, the outcomes in activities outside the gym may be far superior.

Foundation canine behaviors for cross training

For the purpose of the cross training exercises in this book, there are a number of foundation behaviors that will increase neural encoding for an optimal conditioning experience. Teaming up with a certified dog trainer who has a working knowledge of shaping will help teach a dog these behaviors prior to beginning a conditioning program. Please see the download-to-own video *Shaping for Fitness* at www.caninefitnesszone.com for demonstrations of these cues and behaviors.

- "Sit," "Wait" and "Release" cues
- Nose targeting

Nose targeting

- Paw targeting

Paw targeting

- Independent front feet movement

Independent front feet movement

- Independent back feet movement

Independent back feet movement

Foundation human behaviors for cross training

For many individuals, the most challenging element of starting a cross training program for a dog is the human element. Most people have to learn patience while training the dog motor learning exercises for quality neural encoding. Simply placing the dog on the equipment sounds fast and simple. For the sake of the dog's fitness level, it is best to not allow yourself to get inpatient and frustrated and attempt the hasty road to success. Instead, take the slow, methodical cross training road that includes shaping as the primary training method. If this path is taken, common human mistakes including not completing the fitness tests, placing the dog on the equipment and ignoring the importance of good form and control can be avoided. All of these mistakes can weaken the dog's motor learning and can prevent quality neural encoding which decreases the probability of carry over into other activities.

During a cross training session, if you get aggravated (and you will), step back and take a good look at your dog. Inside those bright eyes he's trying his best to learn something new. As he's trying, his heart is racing, nerves are changing and muscles pumping. He loves this stuff. He deserves the opportunity to do it right. Take a break. Come back tomorrow. A happy and relaxed dog loves to learn.

CHAPTER 3

Balance

Canine Cross Training Spotlight

Name: Idgie (the dog doing the exercises and featured in the photos below)
Owner: Sarah
Age: Three
Breed: Border Collie

DVM Observations: Cleared for a conditioning program.

Conditioning Goal: Highly competitive agility dog. Needs to be fast and injury-free to compete at an international level.

CCRT Observations: Will benefit from working up to Level Four balance, strength and endurance exercises:

- Balance exercises to strengthen core and increase body awareness for faster reaction times.

- Strength exercises to increase speed off the start line and decreases the probability of injuries.

- Endurance sprint training to increase speed.

- Stretching with the agility stretching routine found in *The Healthy Way to Stretch Your Dog* after every session of exercises.

- Recommend quarterly sports physicals to identify soft tissue imbalances long before they manifest as potential injuries The CCRT will communicate directly with the DVM to discuss any recommendations that require skilled rehabilitation services, including sports physicals.

Building balance

Balance is the first and most important conditioning component in a cross training program. **Balance** is the body's ability to know where it is in the environment and to respond accordingly. Its purpose is both defensive, protecting the body from injury and offensive, helping the body fine-tune movements. This occurs because the body provides the brain with three types of sensory input that help delineate body position: (1) visual, from the eyes; (2) vestibular, from the ears; and (3) sensory, from the muscles and tendons (Kandel, et. al., 1991). The brain integrates these sensations creating a picture of where the body is in relation to the physical world. If the position feels unstable or unsafe, the brain sends an action signal to the muscles and the body employs fine-tuning movements to protect itself from injury.

As Idgie steps onto the peanut, her eyes watch, vestibular system senses, and paws feel the movement. This sensory information is sent to the brain where an action decision is made and she either continues the exercise or steps off the equipment.

Because balance results from integration of vision, inner ear balance and touch, training each of the systems will improve balance. The opposite is also true. If even one of these three systems is not functioning optimally, balance may be impaired. Older dogs with visual or vestibular impairments may hesitate to jump down or move quickly. Athletic dogs with decreased rear limb awareness may demonstrate imprecise movement. Young dogs, still sculpting their nervous systems, may simply lie down to prevent falling. Fortunately, all three of these systems can be trained to function at their greatest capacity, in particular the sensory system which can be maximized in healthy dogs using balance training exercises that include core stabilization and whole body awareness.

Building core stability

As the dog's **core stability** improves, balance reactions also improve. Increasing core stability requires strengthening **postural stabilizing muscles** also known as the core stabilizers. Unlike the long muscles that move the limbs, postural stabilizing muscles hold the body upright. In general, they are smaller, spanning near or over joints. They contain a high density of **proprioceptive fibers**, nerves that send body position signals to the brain (Martin, et. al., 1991). Strengthening these muscles increases the quality of information the brain receives as well as optimizing the body's ability to respond to brain decisions (Ghez, et. al., 1991). Strengthening the postural stabilizing muscles of the low back, including the abdominal muscles, creates a corset-like effect that controls movement in this highly mobile area of the spine (Herbert, et. al., 2010). Good control of the low back provides a solid center in the body from which all limb movement emanates. Without a strong core, the low back can become hypermobile, predisposing a dog to back injuries and decreasing the quality of front and rear limb movement.

The strength gained with core stabilization exercises, if done with high quality and good form, will carry over into many different activities. Copper demonstrates Level 3 core stabilization strength with beautifully controlled hip extension (in the first photo). Notice how the strength gained carries over into vertical jumping, an activity that Copper does daily chasing squirrels along an eight foot fence line.

Balance builds whole body awareness

Another benefit of building balance is improved **whole body awareness**. Whole body awareness exercises increase the rate, or speed, of **limb reaction time**. Fast reaction time allows for precise movement changes on the fly, helping a dog navigate uneven terrain or quickly change directions at high speeds. Improvement in reaction time can only occur if the dog is consciously aware of all four limbs and is able to move them independently. If limb awareness is limited in the rear limbs, for example, movement may be cumbersome and disordered. This limits the quantity and quality of the signals the brain receives so balance reaction decisions are based on partial information about body position. Increasing limb reaction time with whole body awareness exercises helps dogs become aware of their entire bodies translating into conscious four-limb movement. (An interesting side note. It appears that dogs who learn to use their back legs independently start to have a preference for independent back limb movement during exercise.)

Balance exercises improve the strength of postural stabilizing muscles and increase the rate of limb reaction time. When completed consistently with good form, they provide the brain with precise sensory information about limb location. In turn, more accurate signals are sent to the body so positional changes can be fast and exact. This can help decrease the probability of a geriatric dog falling down, an athlete sustaining a sporting injury or a playful puppy tripping. It is the first and most important conditioning component in a cross training program.

Balance tests

In order for balance to improve, the exercises must be difficult enough in terms of overload principle for the nerves and muscles to begin the process of cellular adaptation, remapping new nerve pathways to create new movement patterns, but not so difficult that the dog has to compensate while completing the exercises (which leads to lower quality movement patterns). So in order to start the dog off with the exercises that will promote maximum benefit, core stabilization and whole body awareness tests must be completed. How a dog performs on these tests determine which balance exercise level he should begin with.

Core stabilization and whole body awareness testing

There are four levels each of testing for core stabilization and whole body awareness, numbered one to four. The core stabilization tests determine how long the dog can maintain a position in which his rear feet are placed on a piece of exercise equipment. The higher the rear legs are raised, the more difficult it is to maintain the position. A dog with good core strength, all things being equal, will be able to maintain the position a relatively long time and can begin his training with more difficult balance exercises. The whole body awareness tests involve placing the dog's rear feet on an unstable surface (wobble board, tilt board) to determine how steady he is on the object and how long he can remain on it.

To prepare to build the balance component of a dog's cross training program, look at the Balance Training Calendar below. This calendar tracks the balance exercise in terms of intensity, frequency and duration and provides a schedule on which to mark down when the exercises have been completed. Begin by testing the dog for core stabilization and whole body awareness. When the exercise levels are determined, mark the levels on the Balance Training Calendar. When you have completed the tests for the other conditioning components, strength and endurance in the following chapters, then read Chapter 6, Activity Specific Cross Training Programs. This chapter will describe precisely which exercises should be included in a dog's conditioning program and what the conditioning goal should be for specific activities.

Balance Training Calendar

Frequency: Twice a week
Intensity: Core, 5 reps; WBA, 10 reps
Duration: Twelve weeks
Goal:

Exercise	Current Level				1	2	3	4	5	6	7	8	9	10	11	12	
Core Stability	1	2	3	4													re-test
Whole Body Awareness	1	2	3	4													

Balance training calendar. (Large format available on page 122.)

Level One and Two core stabilization tests
Ask the dog to stand with his rear feet on a balance disc. He can do this by walking over the top of the disc so that his front feet are on the floor while his rear feet remain on the disc or by asking him to step backward onto the disc, then rewarding him. Test to see if the dog can hold the position for fifteen seconds and repeat five times. If the brain receives a signal that the body is able to maintain the position, even if it is difficult, the nerves will signal the muscles to remain on the disc. This position will be maintained until the muscles fatigue and cause the dog to step off the disc. If the dog is very unsteady and/or repetitively steps off the disc, begin the core stabilization exercises at Level One. If the dog is unsteady but keeps his feet on the disc, begin exercises at Level Two. If the dog is stable and can complete the exercise for five repetitions, then have him perform the Level Three

test below. This process continues until the correct intensity of exercise is determined. Once the correct exercises are chosen, they should be completed for twice a week for twelve weeks. Please see specific exercises later in this chapter for number of repetitions per session.

Level One and Two core stabilization test.

Level Three core stabilization test

Ask the dog to stand with his rear feet on an elbow-height box. He can do this by walking over the top of the box so that his front feet are on the floor while his rear feet remain on the box or by asking him to step backward onto the disc, then reward. Hold fifteen seconds, and repeat five times. If the dog is very unsteady and/or repetitively steps off the box, begin the core stabilization exercises at Level Two. If the dog is unsteady but keeps his feet on the box for fifteen seconds, begin the exercises at Level Three. If the dog can complete the exercise with good stability for five repetitions of fifteen seconds, test for Level Four.

Level Three core stabilization test.

Level Four core stabilization test

Ask the dog to stand with his rear feet on an elbow-height peanut by having him to step backwards onto the peanut. At this level, the dog must have independent rear limb movement to safely complete Level Four core stabilization exercises. Hold fifteen seconds and repeat five times. If the dog is very unsteady and/or repetitively steps off the peanut, begin the core exercises at Level Three. If the dog is unsteady but keeps his feet on the peanut, begin the exercises at Level Four. If the dog can complete the exercise with good stability, then contact *Canine Fitness Zone* for elite Level Five conditioning exercises. Note that the recommended peanut height for this exercise is much lower than what is recommended by some equipment companies. For toy and mini breeds, turning a balance stone upside-down will provide the same exercise intensity at the correct equipment height.

Level Four core stabilization test.

The following diagram provides an illustration of the core stabilization testing process.

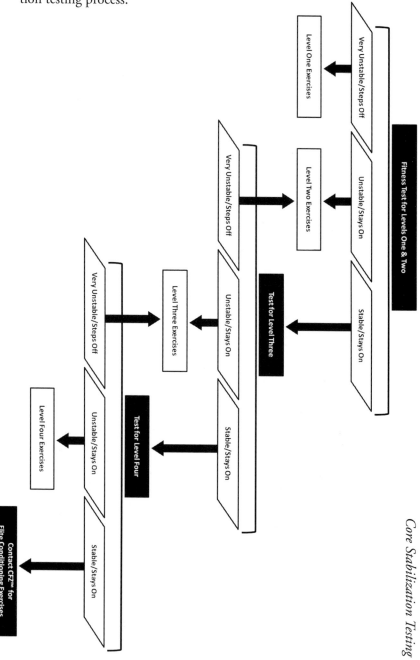

Canine Cross Training Spotlight

Idgie takes the balance test for core stabilization

In the photo above, Idgie is taking the balance tests for core stabilization and whole body awareness. She tests into core stabilization Level Three exercises and whole body awareness Level Four exercises. Because all exercises require a strong core, she will begin all exercises with whole body awareness and strength exercises (see Chapter 4), at the core stabilization Level Three or lower. She will complete these exercises for twelve weeks, twice a week. If she is competing in agility trials consecutive weekends she will follow the *Canine Fitness Zone* Hojo motto. (Coined by Chris Holmquist-Johnson in the *4-Tiered Athletic Conditioning* Seminar, "Well, if you have to rest forty-eight hours before a competition and forty-eight hours after, that would mean you'd train twice a week or...Wednesdays.") "Twice a week or Wednesdays" will complete the exercises only once in the middle of the week allowing her body time to rest before competition and recover after competition. When she begins training, she can only hold the core stabilization exercises for five seconds (the goal is five repetitions of fifteen seconds). This is acceptable. Over the course of the next twelve weeks her balance will progressively improve.

Level One and Two whole body awareness tests

Ask the dog to place his front feet on a wobble board and reward. If the dog is very unsteady and repetitively steps off the board, begin the exercises at Level One. If the dog is unsteady and remains on the board, but has difficulty controlling the movement, begin exercises at Level Two. If the dog is steady and remains on the board easily maneuvering it in all directions, complete the test for Level Three.

Level One and Two whole body awareness tests.

Level Three whole body awareness test

Ask the dog to place all of his feet on the tilt board positioned to shift from right to left and reward. If the dog is very unsteady and/ or repetitively steps off the board, begin the exercises at Level Two. If the dog is unsteady and remains on the board, but has difficulty moving the board or controlling the movement, begin exercises at Level Three. If dog is steady and remains on board easily maneuvering it in both directions, complete the test for Level Four.

Level Three whole body awareness test.

Level Four whole body awareness test

Ask the dog to place all of his feet on wobble board and reward. If the dog is very unsteady and/or repetitively steps off the board, begin awareness exercises at Level Three. If the dog is unsteady and remains on the board but has difficulty moving the board or controlling the movement, begin the exercises at Level Four. If the dog remains on the board and easily maneuvers the board in all directions, contact *Canine Fitness Zone* (www.caninefitnesszone.com) for elite Level Five conditioning exercises.

Level Four whole body awareness test.

Core stabilization and whole body awareness exercises

When core stabilization and whole body awareness exercises are initiated, a series of events take place in the nervous system that, over a twelve week period, improves the accuracy of balance reactions. (Please see Chapter 4 for cellular adaptation of strength training.) For example, when a dog begins core stabilization exercises on the balance disc, the following series of nervous system events occur: (1) the muscles of the hip contract to move the rear limbs onto the disc; (2) as the muscles contract they move the joint; (3) as the joint changes position, the nerves around the joint, including the nerves of postural stabilizing muscles, send signals to the brain; (4) the brain combines these signals with visual and vestibular input; (5) the brain integrates these signals and determines if the body needs to change positions or not; (6) the brain sends the signal to the body; and (7) the body responds. When the exercises are completed with good posture and control, the nerves and muscles adapt so balance reactions become more efficient.

Training specificity

The principle of training specificity states that balance exercises will improve balance, not strength, endurance or flexibility. Because core stabilization requires strengthening the postural stabilizing muscles, it is considered a strengthening exercise as well as a balance exercise and it is placed in the balance chapter because it is the foundation of all movement. Without a strong core, limb movement can cause hyper-mobility of the back predisposing the dog to chronic pain and injury, fast balance reactions can never occur and rear limb strength can never carry over into performance activities. The importance of building powerful core strength is the reason it is the most significant component in a cross training program. To repeat, it is both a balance exercise and a strengthening exercise.

Because core exercises strengthen postural stabilizing muscles during the process of training, the body may release lactic acid, a sign that the muscles are strengthening. This causes tight or stiff movement called **delayed—onset—muscle—soreness** (DOMS) twenty-four to forty-eight hours after the exercise. (Please see the Chapter 4 for ways to decrease DOMS in a cross training program). DOMS is the reason balance training should not occur forty-eight hours before an event. Sore and tight muscles can temporarily decrease reaction time.

Whole body awareness, on the other hand, is a true balance exercise. It does not necessarily improve strength, endurance or flexibility. Its purpose is to increase the speed and precision of limb movement by increasing **proprioception**, the signals from the muscles that define body position for the brain. When proprioception is optimized, the body automatically makes fast accurate motor decisions that carry over into many activities.

Balance exercises

Before beginning core stabilization and whole body exercises to improve balance, the correct intensity of exercises must be determined. To determine the appropriate level, begin by asking the dog to complete the Level Two tests detailed above. If the dog is very unsteady or is unable to complete five repetitions of the exercise with good form and control, begin the dog with Level One exercises. If the dog is unsteady but able to complete five repetitions of exercise, begin the dog at Level Two. If the dog is steady and easily completes five repetitions of exercise, test the dog for Level Three. Repeat this process until the correct level is determined. Testing results may place the dog in one level for core stabilization and another level for whole body awareness. Because core stability is the foundation for all movement, all exercises should default to the core stability level.

After balance exercises have been completed for twelve weeks, conditioning outcomes must be reviewed. If the balance goal has been met, the current exercises should continue. If the balance goal has not been met, then the balance exercise intensity should be increased by moving the dog to the next level of exercise. When a dog has progressed to the next level, the twelve week process of cellular adaptation begins again at the start of the new level. At the end of the next twelve week mark, the conditioning outcome should be reviewed again. This process continues until the desired balance outcome has been achieved.

Level One core stabilization exercise

Ask the dog to stand with his back feet behind an immovable object and stretch forward using a nose target. If the dog steps over the object, repeat and stretch forward only as far as the dog can hold the position. Hold for fifteen seconds. Repeat five times. Ensure good posture by insisting on a straight back, eyes looking forward, and maintaining equal weight on the right and left paws.

Level One core stabilization exercise.

Is this too easy?

Isn't this exercise too easy? One of the primary core stabilizing muscles is the Iliopsoas muscle. It spans beneath the spine from the inside upper thigh to the rib cage. In a standing position, with the body stretched forward, this muscle has to eccentrically contract (control the movement as the muscle lengthens) to maintain the position. If the dog steps out of this stacked position easily, it is highly likely this primary core stabilizing muscle is weak or tight. Including Iliopsoas stretches in the post-exercise stretch routine will help optimize this muscle's extensibility for improved core stabilization strength.

Level Two core stabilization exercise

Ask the dog to stand with his back feet on a balance disc by having him step forward over the disc or step backward onto the disc. Ask him to stretch forward using nose targeting. If the dog steps off the disc, repeat and stretch forward only as far as the dog can hold the position. Hold for fifteen seconds. Repeat five times. Ensure good posture by insisting on a straight back, eyes looking forward and maintaining equal weight on the right and left paws.

Level Two core stabilization exercise.

Level Three core stabilization exercise

Ask the dog to stand with his back feet on an elbow-height box by having him step forward over the box or step backward onto the box. Ask him to stretch forward using nose targeting. If the dog steps off the box, repeat and stretch forward only as far as the dog can hold the position. Hold for fifteen seconds. Repeat five times. Ensure good posture by insisting on a straight back, eyes looking forward, and maintaining equal weight on the right and left paws. As the dog gets stronger with this exercise, he may choose to roll onto the top of his feet. This is fine as long as good posture is maintained.

Level Three core stabilization exercise.

What if he does not like it?

My dog does not like this exercise. What should I do?

Natural conformation for some dogs includes a sloping croup, or top line, similar to this Whippet. For dogs with this posture, they may be more comfortable completing the exercise on a lower box which doesn't require as much **lumbo-sacral extension,** or arching of the low back.

Level Four core stabilization exercise

Stabilize an elbow-height balance peanut from behind with a box or the wall. Ask the dog to stand with his back feet on the peanut by stepping backward. If the dog steps off the peanut repeat until he can hold the position. Hold for fifteen seconds. Repeat five times. Good posture is still required (straight back, eyes looking forward, and equal weight shifting through the right and left paws). Unlike the exercises in Level One to Three, the dog must actively move the entire body to control the peanut. The exercise is dynamic which can be seen by Idgie's tail movement.

Level Four core stabilization exercise.

Canine Cross Training Spotlight

Idgie enjoying a stretch after exercise

The day following a cross training session, Idgie takes longer leisurely stretches before she gets moving in the morning, an indication she may have DOMS. To decrease muscle stiffness, Sarah takes her for a long walk. The second day after the session, Idgie still seems to be a little stiff and she has to help teach agility class. Before class begins, Sarah makes sure Idgie completes a dynamic warm-up that includes fifteen minutes of walking followed by two repetitions of each exercise before class begins. A dynamic warm-up, one that moves the body increasing circulation and priming the nerves for quick movements, may improve dexterity. This is true for humans, too. See Lori Hansen's *Human Agility Training* to warm-up with your dog. After class Sarah stretches Idgie with the agility stretching routine from *The Healthy Way to Stretch Your Dog*. Static stretching before an event may decrease the passive energy stored in a muscle and therefore decrease strength.

Level One whole body awareness exercise

Ask the dog to place his front feet on a tilt board positioned so it shifts from right to left and reward. Using nose targeting, ask the dog to shift weight from side to side, and reward after each independent shift. Shift ten times. Repeat five times. Keep the dog's hocks parallel to the floor (not allowing the dog to put the rear feet close to the tilt board) to engage the core. Ensure good posture (straight back, eyes looking forward, and equal weight on the right and left paws).

Level One whole body awareness exercise.

Level Two whole body awareness exercise

Ask the dog to place his front feet on the wobble board and reward. Using nose targeting, ask the dog to shift his weight from side to side then front and back, rewarding after each independent shift. Shift ten times each side to side and front to back. Repeat five times. Keep the dog's hocks parallel to the floor (not allowing the dog to put the rear feet close to the tilt board) to engage the core. Ensure good posture (straight back, eyes looking forward, equal weight shift on the right and left paws).

Level Two whole body awareness exercise.

Level Three whole body awareness exercise

Ask the dog to place all of his feet on the tilt board positioned to shift from right to left and reward. Using nose targeting, ask the dog to shift from side to side and reward after each independent shift. Shift ten times side to side. Repeat five times. For Level Three and Four exercises, the dog will engage the core by rounding the back to get all his paws on the board. This active flexion, or rounding, of the lumbar spine or low back contracts the core stabilizing muscles creating a strong anchor for the limbs as they attempt to control the board. His eyes should gaze toward the floor to maintain a comfortable spine alignment. Weight shifting is dynamic and is not expected to be equal right to left until the dog understands the exercise at which time he should shift the board smoothly from right to left with good control.

Level Three whole body awareness exercise.

Level Four whole body awareness exercise

Ask the dog to place all of his feet on the wobble board and reward. Using nose targeting, ask him to shift his weight in a circle touching all edges of the board to the floor. Initially use nose targeting to teach him to shift from side to side, front to back and reward after each independent shift. Work up to shifting ten times in a circle. Repeat five times. For Level Four exercises, the dog will engage the core by rounding the back to get all paws on the board. This active flexion, or rounding of the lumbar spine or low back, contracts the core stabilizing muscles creating a strong anchor for the limbs as they attempt to control the board. His eyes should gaze toward the floor to maintain a comfortable spine alignment. Weight shifting is dynamic and is not expected to be equal right to left until the dog understands the exercise.

Level Four whole body awareness exercise.

Canine Cross Training Spotlight

Idgie completing Level Four exercises

At the end of her first twelve weeks of cross training, Idgie again completes the core stabilization and whole body awareness tests. This time she tests into Level Four for both exercises. She begins the new exercises on week thirteen. She will complete these exercises for twelve weeks, twice a week. The goal for core stabilization is to hold the exercise for fifteen seconds, five repetitions. When she initiates the exercises she is immediately able to hold each for ten seconds, an indication that her core strength has improved enough to hold the position and her nerve reactions are fast enough to calibrate movements. At the end of Level Four training, she will contact *Canine Fitness Zone* for Level Five elite level conditioning exercises.

Equipment Sizing

Large breeds should be able to use standard sized tilt and wobble boards.

Initially, it may be challenging to get all four paws on the board since they must have very strong abdominal muscles in order to do so. As they are learning the exercise, they may attempt to compensate as Breaker is doing here by grabbing the front of the board with his toes. By doing this, he is attempting to control the board with his paws. In time he will learn to place his feet flat on the board. Giant breed dogs may benefit from larger sized boards which can be special ordered at www.caninefitnesszone. com.

Knowledge Assessment, True or False

Visual, vestibular and sensory integration help with balance? True.

Balance training can occur on the same day as strength and endurance training? True.

Balance training can improve limb reaction time? True.

CHAPTER 4

Strength

Canine Cross Training Spotlight

Name: Breaker
Owner: Ashley
Age: Five

Breed: Doberman Pincher

DVM Observations: Cleared for a conditioning program.

Conditioning Goal: Get into top condition in three months for a national conformation dog show. Increase rear limb definition while maintaining balanced conformation. Other activities include demonstration dog for tricks class, obedience and agility.

CCRT Observations: While conditioning for the show, it is recommended Breaker take a break from competitive agility. Conditioning to meet his conformation goal increases muscle bulk and therefore weight. Conditioning to meet an agility goal leans out muscles and decreases weight and this lower agility weight decreases forces on the body that may predispose a dog to injury. Focus on:

- Core stability to strengthen top line and increase reach and drive.

- Rear limb strength exercises to increase rear limb muscle definition.

- Front limb strength exercises to maintain balanced conformation and prevent bulk over the shoulder (which will occur if Level Three or Four front limb exercises are completed).

- Endurance exercises, short sprints only, to increase thigh muscle bulk.

- Perform the conformation stretching routine in *The Healthy Way to Stretch Your Dog* after each session of exercise.

Building strength

Strength exercises build power in muscles so the body can move. For most activities, muscles move the body weight through a set of actions. Specific actions require strength in particular muscles. For example, dock diving requires core and rear limb strength to increase jump distance and decrease the probability of back injuries. Lure coursing requires core, front limb and rear limb strength to balance the "spring" action of running. Flyball requires core, front limb and back limb strength to push off the box and decrease the probability of carpal (wrist) injuries (Jaeger and Canapp, 2008). When strength meets or exceeds the power requirements of an activity, movement is fluid and graceful. When strength requirements are insufficient, movement is too tight or too loose and the body is at risk for injury.

Conditioning principles in strength training

All muscle contractions are not the same. They are graded to meet the demands of a specific activity. When the body steps forward, a small amount of force is needed to complete the task. When the body jumps forward, a larger amount of force is needed. This ability to modulate force for differing activities is a function of the motor unit (Duchateau and Enocha, 2011). A **motor unit** is a single motor neuron and all of the corresponding muscle fibers it **innervates** or communicates with. Each muscle has many motor units, allowing the brain to grade power requirements for specific activities. This is important for strength training because, in order to produce enough overload to begin cellular adaptation, many motor units must be activated to generate a high force muscle contraction. This is called **maximizing motor unit recruitment** and it must be achieved to increase power in the muscle (Shalit, et. al., 2011).

Strength tests

In order to increase strength, exercises must be challenging enough for the muscles to begin the process of cellular adaptation, but not so difficult that the body compensates in some counter-productive way. To determine the correct exercise intensity level, strength tests are required. The results of these tests determine the dog's current strength, making it possible to determine which level of exercise should be initiated.

There are eight strength tests, four levels each for the front and rear limbs. Strength testing each of these primary areas ensures the dog will be able to complete exercises with correct amount of overload. Each of the tests measures the ability of the dog to maintain his position on either an unstable surface or with his front or rear limbs elevated.

Completing front limb and rear limb exercises requires the core to be strong enough to stabilize the body. Sometimes a dog's front and rear limb strength test levels will score higher than his core level. For example, the front limb strength scores at Level Three, the rear limb at Level Four and core at Level Two. This means you will need to lower the front and rear limb exercises to Level Two to prevent compensation by the core stabilizing muscles that can predispose the entire body to muscular imbalances. When the correct level is determined, the exercises should be completed for twelve weeks, two times per week, with ten high quality repetitions of each exercise.

To prepare to build the strength component of a dog's cross training program, look at the Strength Training Calendar below. This calendar clarifies the strength exercise, intensity, frequency and duration, and then provides a schedule on which to mark down when the exercises have been completed. With the calendar close by, begin by testing the dog for front and rear limb strength. When the exercise levels are determined, mark the levels on the Strength Training Calendar. When you have completed the tests for the last conditioning component, endurance in the following chapter, read Chapter 6, Activity Specific Cross Training Programs. This chapter will describe precisely which exercises should be included in a dog's conditioning program and what level is recommended for specific activities.

Strength Training Calendar

Frequency: Twice a week
Intensity: Ten controlled repetitions
Duration: Twelve weeks/eight weeks
Goal:

	Exercise	Current Level				1	2	3	4	5	6	7	8	9	10	11	12	
Front Limb	Side-stepping	1	2	3	4													re-test
	Push-ups	1	2	3	4													
Rear Limb	Side-stepping	1	2	3	4													
	Sit-to-stand	1	2	3	4													

Strength training calendar (Large format available on page 123.)

Level One and Two strength tests for front limbs
Place two balance stones slightly wider than the dog's shoulder width. Ask the dog to step up onto the stones and reward. With the dog's front paws on the stones, ask the dog to nose target toward the

floor into a push-up position and reward. Repeat five times. If the dog is unable to complete this exercise with a straight back and good control, begin with Level One exercises. If the dog is able to complete the exercise with a straight back and good control but steps off or is unsteady, begin with Level Two exercises. If the dog is able to complete the exercise with a straight back and good control for ten repetitions, test for Level Three.

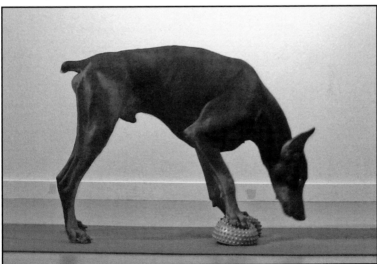

Level One and Two strength tests for front limbs.

Level Three strength test for front limbs

Place the elbow-height box on a non-skid surface. Ask the dog to step onto the box with all four feet. Reward. Ask the dog to place his front feet on the floor keeping his back feet on the box. Reward. With his back feet remaining on the box, ask him to nose target toward the floor into a push-up position and reward. Repeat five times. If the dog is unable to complete the exercise with a straight back and good control, begin with Level Two exercises. If the dog is able to complete the exercise with a straight back and good control but steps off or is unsteady, begin with Level Three exercises. If able to complete with straight back and good control for ten repetitions, test for Level Four.

Level Three strength test for front limbs.

Level Four strength test for front limbs

Ask the dog to place his hind feet on an elbow-height box and his front feet on the balance stones and reward. Ask the dog to nose target toward the floor into push-up position and reward. Repeat five times. If the dog is unable to complete the exercise with a straight back and good control, begin with Level Three exercises. If the dog is able to complete the exercise with a straight back and good control but steps off or is unsteady, begin with Level Four exercises. If the dog is able to complete the exercise with a straight back and good control for ten repetitions, contact *Canine Fitness Zone* for elite Level Five exercises.

Level Four strength test for front limbs.

Level One and Two strength tests for hind limbs

Ask the dog to sit in front of a balance disc and reward. Ask the dog to place his front paws on the balance disc and reward. Keeping front paws on the balance disc, ask the dog to stand and reward. Complete five repetitions. If the dog is unable to complete the exercise with a straight back and good control, begin with Level One exercises. If the dog is able to complete the exercise with a straight back and good control, but is unsteady or unable to complete five repetitions, begin with Level Two exercises. If the dog is able to complete the exercise with a straight back and good control for ten repetitions, test for Level Three.

Level One and Two strength tests for hind limbs.

Level Three strength test for hind limbs

Ask the dog to sit in front of an elbow-height box and reward. Ask the dog to place his front paws on an elbow-height box and reward. Keeping the front paws on the box, ask the dog to stand and reward. Complete five repetitions. If the dog is unable to complete the exercise with a straight back and good control, begin with Level Two exercises. If the dog is able to complete the exercise with a straight back and good control, but steps off or is unable to complete five repetitions, begin with Level Three exercises. If the dog is able to complete the exercise with a straight back and good control for ten repetitions, test for Level Four.

Level Three strength test for hind limbs.

Level Four strength test for hind limbs

Stabilize the elbow-height peanut against a box or wall. Ask the dog to sit in front of the peanut and reward. Ask the dog to place his front paws on the peanut and reward. Keeping the front paws on the peanut, ask the dog to stand and reward. Similar to the Level Four Core stabilization exercise, this exercise is very dynamic, requiring the dog to use his core stabilizing muscles to control the movement of the ball while doing a squat. Complete five repetitions. If the dog is unable to complete the exercise with a straight back and good dynamic control (the peanut is staying beneath the paws not rolling across the room), begin with Level Three exercises. If the dog is able to complete the exercise with a straight back and good control, but steps off or is unable to complete five repetitions, begin with Level Four exercises. If the dog is able to complete the exercise with a straight back and good control for ten repetitions, contact *Canine Fitness Zone* for elite Level Five exercises.

Level Four strength test for hind limbs.

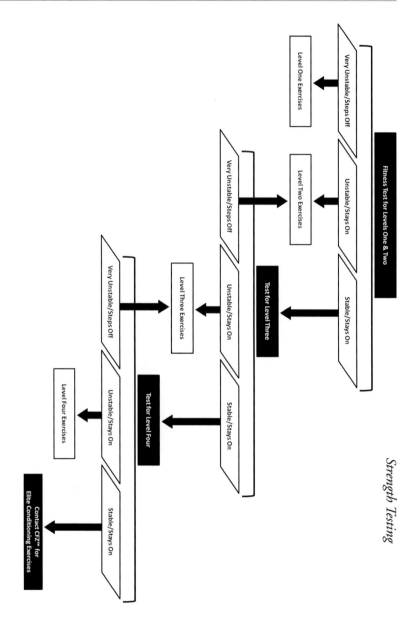

Strength Testing

Canine Cross Training Spotlight

Breaker tested into Level Two core stabilization exercises

Prior to taking the front and rear limb strength tests, Breaker completed the core stabilization test (see Chapter 3). He tested into Level Two core stabilization exercises. He tests into Level Three front limb exercises and Level Three rear limb exercises. Because all exercises require a strong core, he will begin all exercises at Level Two (which is as high as he should go for front limb strengthening for conformation because Levels Three and Four may increase bulk over the shoulder). The balance and strength components of his program will consist of Level Two core stabilization, front limb and rear limb exercises. He will complete these exercises for twelve weeks, twice a week, ten repetitions of each exercise with good posture and control. For conformation dogs, good posture means special emphasis should be placed on maintaining the top line while completing the exercises.

Strength training phases

There are three phases of cellular adaptation for strength training: **motor unit activation; cellular strengthening;** and the **plateau**

(Wilmore and Costill, 2005). When strength training exercises are initiated, if the correct level of exercises is used, the physiological process of increasing motor unit recruitment begins. At first the nerves are not very efficient at getting to the motor units and the motor units are not very proficient at receiving the message. Over the course of about four weeks, the nerves synchronize with the muscles, making communication between the nerves and muscles more effective. It is at this point in the strength training program when the first improvements in muscle tone and movement quality can be seen. These physical improvements are more likely due to an increase in motor unit recruitment, not an increase in strength at the cellular level which is required to increase the amount of force a muscle can produce (Gabriel, et. al., 2006.)

The second phase of cellular adaptation, cellular strengthening, occurs deep inside the muscle cells. A muscle cell is comprised of filaments which are long bands of tubular structures. Filaments are arranged parallel to each other and produce force, or strength, by chemically binding with each other. The more and the tighter the chemical bonds, the more force a muscle produces. The cells can be coaxed into increasing the number and strength of their bonds by completing exercises that provide an adequate amount of overload. As a muscle completes an exercise, the muscle filaments bond together. If the bonds are strong and the dog has enough strength to complete the exercise with ease the exercise is too easy. If the bonds are not strong enough and the muscle fails, then the dog does not have enough strength to complete the exercise meaning it can be judged to be too hard. If the bonds are strong but they fatigue during the course of the exercise, the proper amount of overload has been achieved and the process of cellular adaptation will signal the body to increase the number and strength of the chemical bonds.

When a strength training program is initiated, the physiological process of cellular adaptation takes approximately twelve weeks of training twice a week with ten repetitions completed with good control. During this time, as exercises are completed, lactic acid will be released causing delayed-onset muscle soreness (DOMS) approximately forty eight hours after the training session. It can make movement look and feel stiff and tight. Lactic acid release in the muscles cannot be prevented during a strength training program, but some of it can be decreased by increasing circulation with endurance exercises. DOMS is the reason strength training should be halted forty eight hours before a competition or event; it can temporarily impact movement. If competing in events every weekend, choosing to follow the *Canine Fitness Zone* Hojo motto, "Twice a week or Wednesdays," will ensure overload is being met without putting the dog at risk for overtraining.

> ## Canine Cross Training Spotlight
> About four weeks into the program Ashley notices a significant improvement in flexibility during Breaker's post-exercise stretching routine. At the same time he is self-stretching more the morning following an exercise session, an indication that he may be experiencing DOMS. This is most likely because his improvement in flexibility is allowing him to strengthen portions of the muscle that have probably not been strengthened before. Soreness is a sign that he is consistently maximizing motor unit recruitment for a good strength training effect.

The third phase of cellular adaptation, the **plateau**, occurs at approximately twelve weeks. At this point, motor unit recruitment is optimized increasing the efficiency of nerve signals which enhance the precision of muscle modulation; the body is more efficient at contracting precise muscles with exacting force. Just as important, because the chemical bonds in the muscle are stronger, the muscles can now produce a higher force. The combination of these two physiological changes makes the muscles more powerful and their actions more precise. The body moves through the exercises with grace and ease which carries over into other activities.

Training specificity

The principle of specificity states that strength training will build strength, not endurance, flexibility or balance. Strength gains can improve movement quality and it can also help the body overcome any reasonable external force. For example, if a dog is making a tight turn on a wet surface and his front limb slips out from beneath him, the muscles on the inside of the shoulder contract in an attempt to counter the force. If the muscles are strong enough, they overcome the force preventing the limb from slipping further and the dog makes the turn without sustaining an injury. If the muscles are not strong enough, they won't overcome the force. In this case, the limbs tend to slip, predisposing the muscle, ligament and joint to injury. Increasing strength on all sides of a joint in areas susceptible to repetitive joint stresses may decrease the probability of these types of injuries (Tsang and DiPasquale, 2011).

Progressing a strength training program

During the twelfth week of strength training, cellular adaptation, and therefore strength, has reached a plateau. The body is capable of completing the exercises with grace and ease. If the strength outcome has been met, the current exercises should continue. If the strength outcome has not been met, the exercise intensity should be increased by moving the dog to the next exercise level. If the dog is moved to the next level, the three phases of cellular adaptation will begin all over again, with one exception. The process of maximizing motor unit activation recruitment has all ready been completed. After the initial twelve week period of strength training, only eight weeks is required to create cellular strength. At the end of this eight week period, the strength outcome will need to be reviewed and the program stabilized or upgraded to the next level as needed.

Canine Cross Training Spotlight

Breaker stops cross training forty-eight hours before he goes to the dog show. His top line is firm from core stabilization exercises, his rear limb muscles are significantly more defined, and his rear limb drive is more powerful. When he returns from competition, after a forty-eight hour rest, he will re-test for all exercises in preparation for agility and obedience training. His new program should include core stabilization, whole-body awareness, front and rear limb strength and short distance sring training (see Chapter 6, Activity Specific Cross Training Programs). The post-exercise stretching routine should be transitioned from the conformation routine to the agility or obedience routine.

Front limb strength exercises

Level One strength exercises for front limbs

Exercise One: Side-stepping. Ask the dog to stand on a mat and reward. Ask the dog to nose target to the side so he has to side step to reach the target and reward. Repeat to the other side. Repeat ten times with the right step and the left step equaling one repetition. Because this is a novel behavior for dogs, it is often one of the harder behaviors to teach. However, it is particularly important for agility dogs who choose to do weave poles by pushing the pole out of the way with one front limb at a time (versus choosing to hop with both front feet at the same time) since this position may place high stresses through the medial joint capsule of the shoulder, predisposing these dogs to medial shoulder instability injuries. This exercise specifically trains the Subscapularis muscle that crosses, and potentially stabilizes, the medial shoulder joint line.

Side-stepping motion required in Level One.

Exercise Two: Push-up on markers. Place two markers on the floor slightly wider than the dog's shoulder width. Ask the dog to place a paw on each marker and reward. Nose target the dog toward the floor so he must bend his elbow and reach his neck forward to hit the target and reward. Repeat ten times.

Exercise Two: Push-up on floor.

Importance of proper push-up form

A play bow, although a common behavior in many dog's repertoires, is bio-mechanically not the same as a push-up. Compare the push-up photo on page 68 to the one above. Notice how, in proper push-up position, the shoulder and elbow joints are flexed (bent). This position puts the muscles in an advantageous position for strengthening. In a play bow, the muscles are not overloaded because the dog is resting the forearms on the floor. This difference can be seen by comparing muscle bulk in these two photos. The shoulder muscles are clearly defined in the photo on page 68 because the muscles are contracting to complete the exercise.

Level Two strength exercises for front limbs

Equipment set-up: Place two balance stones on the floor slightly wider than the dog's shoulder width.

Exercise One. Side step on stones. Ask the dog to place both paws on one stone and reward. Ask the dog to step to the other stone by asking him to nose target to the side and reward. Using a nose target to the other side, ask the dog to step back to the original stone and reward. Repeat ten times, right step and left step equals one repetition.

Exercise One. Side step on stones.

Exercise Two: Push-up on stones. Place two stones on the floor slightly wider than the dog's shoulder width. Ask the dog to place a paw on each stone and reward. Nose target the dog toward the floor so he must bend his elbows and reach his neck forward to hit the target and reward. Repeat ten times.

As with the Level Two front limb strength test, the dog is asked to maintain his feet on the stones except now is asked to touch the floor ten times with his nose.

Muscle Observation

It is obvious from the large arcs of movement in this exercise that it is strengthening the muscles of the shoulder and elbow. But it is also strengthening the carpal (wrist) flexor muscles. As the dog leans forward the muscles on the back of the carpus must contract very strongly to maintain this position.

Level Three strength exercises for front limbs

Exercise One: Back feet on elbow-height box, side step on floor. Ask the dog to place back feet on box and reward. Ask the dog to nose target to the side so he has to side step to reach the target and reward. Repeat on the other side. Repeat ten times with the right step and the left step equaling one repetition.

Exercise One: Back feet on elbow-height box, side step on floor.

Exercise Two: Back feet on elbow-height box, push-up on floor.
Place markers on the floor about half the dog's body length away
from the box and slightly wider than the dog's shoulder width. Ask
the dog to place his back feet on box and reward. Ask the dog to
place his front feet on the markers and reward. Ask the dog to push-
up by nose targeting forward and reward. Repeat ten times.

Exercise Two: Back feet on elbow-height box, push-up on floor.

Level Four strength exercises for front limbs
Exercise One: Back feet on point-of-elbow-height box, side step on stones. Place the balance stones on the floor about half the dog's body length away from the box and slightly wider than the dog's shoulder width. Ask the dog to place his back feet on the box and reward. Ask the dog to place his front feet on the stones and reward. Ask the dog to step from one stone to the next using hand targeting and reward. Repeat ten times. The right step and left step equals one repetition.

Exercise One: Back feet on point-of-elbow-height box, side step on stones.

Exercise Two: Back feet on point-of-elbow-height box, push-up on stones. Place the balance stones on the floor about half the dog's body length away from the box and slightly wider than the dog's shoulder width. Ask the dog to place his back feet on the box and reward. Ask the dog to place his front feet on the stones and reward. Ask the dog to push-up by nose targeting forward and reward. Repeat ten times.

Exercise Two: Back feet on point-of-elbow-height box, push-up on stones.

Hind limb strength exercises

Level One strength exercises for hind limbs
Exercise One: Sit to stand on half elbow-height box. Ask the dog to sit with the front feet on a box that is about half the height of an elbow-height box and reward. Nose target so the dog stands up leaning forward to reach the target and reward. Ask the dog to sit and reward. Repeat ten times.

Exercise One: Sit to stand on half elbow-height box.

How does this work?

If my dog's front paws are on the equipment, why is this strengthening his rear legs? When the dog places the front feet on a higher surface, the body weight is shifted onto the rear legs and the higher the front feet are off the floor and more weight is on the rear limbs. An easy way to feel this is to do a push-up with the front feet on the floor then do a push-up with hands on a table. When the front feet are on the table, the push-up is easier because much of the body weight has shifted back into the legs.

Exercise Two: Side step on half elbow-height box. Ask the dog to stand with his front feet on a box that is about half the height of the elbow-height box and reward. Ask the dog to sidestep with his rear feet (if side stepping isn't yet a learned behavior, stand beside the dog and step into him so he has to side step, reward for the step and repeat. See page 86 for instructions.) Repeat until the dog is side stepping half-way around the box independently. Repeat ten times both ways.

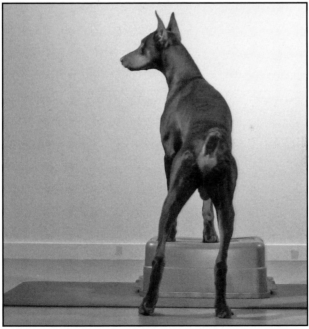

Exercise Two: Side step on half elbow-height box.

Level Two strength exercises for hind limbs

Exercise One: Sit to stand on balance disc. Ask the dog to sit with his front feet on a balance disc and reward. Nose target so the dog stands up leaning forward to reach the target and reward. Ask the dog to sit and reward. Repeat ten times.

Exercise One: Sit to stand on balance disc.

Exercise Two: Side step on balance disc. Ask the dog to stand with his front feet on a balance disc and reward. Ask the dog to sidestep with their rear feet (if side stepping isn't yet a learned behavior, stand beside the dog and step into him so he has to sidestep. Reward for the step and repeat.) Have the dog side step half way around the disc in both directions. Repeat ten times.

Exercise Two: Side step on balance disc.

Level Three strength exercises for hind limbs

Exercise One: Sit to stand on elbow-height box. Ask the dog to sit with the front feet on an elbow-height box and reward. Nose target so the dog stands up leaning forward to reach the target and reward. Ask the dog to sit and reward. Repeat ten times.

Exercise One: Sit to stand on elbow-height box.

Exercise Two: Side step on elbow-height box. Ask the dog to stand with his front feet on an elbow-height box and reward. Ask the dog to sidestep with his rear feet. If the dog requires assistance to stand, stand next to the dog, step into him and provide a verbal cue as you step into him. Reward for side stepping. Step half way around the box both directions. Repeat ten times.

Exercise Two: Side step on elbow-height box.

Level Four strength exercises for hind limbs

Exercise One. Front feet on elbow-height peanut. Ask the dog to sit with the front feet on an elbow-height peanut that is stabilized by a box or wall and reward. Nose target so the dog stands up leaning forward to reach the target and reward. Ask the dog to sit again and reward. Repeat ten times.

Exercise One. Front feet on elbow-height peanut.

Exercise Two. Sidestep around peanut. Ask the dog to stand with his front feet on the peanut that is stabilized with a box or wall and reward. Ask the dog to sidestep half way around peanut in both directions. Repeat ten times.

Exercise Two. Sidestep around peanut.

Knowledge Assessment, True or False

Increasing strength takes eight to twelve weeks. True.

At least forty-eight hours of rest is needed between strength training sessions. True.

Strength training should occur the day before a competitive activity. False.

CHAPTER 5

Endurance

Canine Cross Training Spotlight

Name: Ellie
Age: 5
Breed: Alaskan Husky

Conditioning Goal: High mountain Skijoring for up to four hours, competitive in agility with times of thirty seconds or less.

DVM Observations: Cleared for conditioning program.

CCRT Observations: Decreased rear limb drive. Focus on:

- Strengthen core to build a solid anchor for limb movement.

- Increase whole body awareness for quality movement on uneven terrain.

- Front limb strength exercises to increase front limb pull in skijoring and decrease probability of shoulder injuries in agility.

- Rear limb strength exercises to increase rear limb push in skijoring and increase speed off the start line in agility.

- Short distance sprint training for increased speed in agility.

- Long distance endurance training for skijoring.

- Stretching with the agility stretching routine or the sled pulling routine in *The Healthy Way to Stretch Your Dog* after every bout of exercise

- Recommend quarterly sports physicals to identify soft tissue imbalances long before they manifest as potential injuries.

Building endurance

Endurance provides the body with energy to move. The energy source for cells is **adenosine triphosphate**, or ATP. Muscle cells need ATP like a car needs gasoline. No ATP, no energy to move. But unlike a car, a dog's body has the ability to produce its own ATP. When the gas tank is empty, ATP production begins. In general, ATP production occurs through two different metabolic pathways: **anaerobic**, or without oxygen, for short bursts of energy and sprint distances; and

aerobic, or with oxygen, for long bouts of energy and long distances. These pathways can be trained with endurance exercises to become highly efficient so energy levels can meet or exceed the requirements of any activity.

Before an endurance training program is started, two physical characteristics of the body must be considered. First, core strength (the ability of the abdominal and back muscles to support the center of the body) must be strong. Because endurance exercises require repetitive movement of the limbs, they put additional force through the joints and inter-vertebral discs of the back. Thus a weak core may, over time, lead to degenerative processes in the back. Second, nutrition quality must be high because the first line of energy for all endurance activities is blood sugar and the second line of energy is carbohydrates and fat. These combine to provide the body the energy needed for safe and effective endurance training (Hawley, et. al., 2011).

Proper nutrition is important for all dogs, but is of particular concern for three types of dogs: older dogs; younger dogs; and elite canine athletes. Older dogs may not absorb nutrients or metabolize sugars as well as they once did, placing them at risk for low energy stores particularly if they are exercising beyond their physical abilities. Younger dogs, especially if they are still growing, need energy to build healthy bodies. Asking a puppy to run with a bike, go for a hike or be a distance running partner places too much mechanical and physiological stresses on his growing body. A leisurely romp in the park or a play date with another puppy is a more age-appropriate endurance activity.

Over-exercising puppies and aging dogs is often an unintentional mistake. To prevent over-training, ask yourself approximately how old your dog is in human years. A six month old puppy would be approximately four years old in human terms. A ten year old Lab would be approximately eighty in human years. What exercises might be appropriate for a four-year-old or an eighty-year-old human (taking into consideration baseline fitness level)? These are most likely the most appropriate exercises for your dog. If you have questions, contact a CCRT for age-appropriate exercise options.

Elite athletes may, by virtue of their high level of conditioning, burn as much energy as they consume. For these dogs, when completing endurance exercises, providing high quality snacks that include a mix of carbohydrates, fats and proteins throughout the day will help maintain their energy stores for optimal performance. (Note that the sequence of energy utilization can be breed-specific. Please contact www.caninefitnesszone.com for more information).

Canine Cross Training Spotlight

Ellie has been on a cross training program for six months and has tested into Level Four core stabilization, whole body awareness, front limb strength, and rear limb strength exercises (she began at Level Two and because she followed the program consistently, has now tested into Level Four). Because she is very active on the weekends, she follows the CFZ Hojo motto "twice-a-week-or-Wednesdays" for exercise frequency. Over the summer she took a break from agility and her endurance program consisted primarily of long distance endurance training in the mountains and inconsistent bouts of sprint training such as chasing the ball in a school field. Now that she is ramping up for agility competitions, she needs to increase her sprint training for faster run times. She will continue her high elevation workouts which will include sled pulling and skijoring.

Cellular adaptation during endurance training

Endurance training improves cellular utilization and production of adenoisine triphosphate. This increased production translates into effortless movement for a specified time or a particular distance. For all activities, short distance sprints or long distance run, the physiological process of energy production and utilization is always the same—for the first 30 seconds of movement the body pulls ATP from the anaerobic metabolic pathway and then, if more energy is required, the aerobic metabolic pathway begins to create more ATP through a complicated chemical process (Wilmore and Costill, 2005). By determining which metabolic pathway a dog needs to boost for its particular activity—short distance sprints, intermediate distance sprints or long distance runs—specific endurance exercises can be used for the best activity specific outcomes.

Anaerobic metabolism

When the body needs energy to move, the first place it reaches for is the anaerobic "without-oxygen" metabolic pathway. This pathway produces ATP by accessing **glycogen**, or sugars, in the body. These sugars, if available, are a quick source of energy. But this pathway has two limitations. First, cells carry a finite amount of glycogen. If the body needs to keep moving for more than thirty seconds, it must find another source of energy. It does this by creating its own ATP through the aerobic metabolic pathway. The second limitation is that the anaerobic metabolic pathway creates a chemical by-product called lactic acid that causes a burning sensation in the muscles. When the anaerobic metabolic pathway is trained with proper endurance exercises, the body creates chemicals that buffer this movement-limiting chemical. Human research has shown that lactic acid build-up and slower sprint times are directly correlated (Twist and Eston, 2005). With sprint training, the body is better at managing the by-products of anaerobic metabolism as well as becoming more efficient with utilization of ATP. With these physiological improvements, sprint speeds should get fast as the body becomes for efficient at utilizing the anaerobic metabolic pathway.

Aerobic metabolism

In general, for the first 30 seconds of movement, the body is using ATP from the anaerobic metabolic pathway. During this process the heart begins to beat faster and the rate of respiration increases. These two factors prime the body to begin utilizing the aerobic, "with-oxygen" metabolic pathway. In the ATP producing pathway, oxygen-rich red blood cells travel through the body to the muscle cells. The cells absorb the oxygen and undergo a complicated process to produce ATP. Efficiency of this cycle improves with training because cellular adaptation occurs in four body systems. First, the heart, which is a powerful muscle, becomes stronger. It pumps greater volumes of blood into the body with every contraction. Second, the lungs pull oxygen-rich air deep into the lower lobes improving oxygen absorption from the lungs to the red blood cells. Third, the red blood cells, loaded with oxygen, become more efficient at picking up oxygen and depositing it to the cells. And fourth, the cells become more efficient at converting oxygen into ATP. With these physiological improvements, the body is able to provide itself with energy for extended periods of time allowing for distance sled pulling or fatigue-resistant agility weekends.

Overload for endurance training

To help the body become more efficient at creating and utilizing ATP, it must be pushed to do more intense endurance activities than it is currently doing. Increasing exercise intensity, overloading the body, begins the process of cellular adaptation discussed above. Dogs who compete in various canine sports activities tend to engage in either short sprinting (flyball), intermediate sprinting (agility) or distance running (search and rescue). Training a dog to build up the proper amount of endurance needed will result in optimizing the anaerobic, anaerobic-aerobic or aerobic metabolic pathways respectively. Choosing which type of training a dog needs is simply a matter of determining the amount of time the dog will be moving in its specified activity.

Short sprint, 30 second run time

To improve short sprinting speed, the body must become very efficient at utilizing the anaerobic metabolic pathway whose primary energy source is immediately available blood sugars. Making the anaerobic pathway more efficient can be achieved by short distance sprint endurance training (consecutive repetitions of short sprint distances). For example, if endurance training is initiated to increase speed for agility, determining the correct amount of overload requires measuring the sprint distance of a competitive event and then determining how fast the dog needs to run this distance. Once these two factors are determined, the program can be created including frequency, intensity and duration of the exercise. A training session might consist of running the dog a specified distance while escalating drive, and therefore speed, for each consecutive repetition by increasing the reward. Determining the sprint training distance and the number of repetitions needed to create a training effect is based on the dog's baseline endurance which will be tested before beginning the endurance training sessions. Over a number of weeks, this training may increase the efficiency of the anaerobic pathway and the body will be better able to utilize available sugars for ATP production while buffering lactic acid in the muscles.

Canine Cross Training Spotlight

Ellie loves to chase a soccer ball. This is used as a motivational reward for her short distance sprint training workouts. Because her agility run time goal is thirty seconds, the ball is thrown or kicked across a football field. She is then released to catch the ball. A handler on the other end of the field allows her to catch it then immediately throws it to the other end of the field for a total of thirty seconds of sprint run time. When the time is up, she is released to play with the ball for a few minutes before completing four more sprint training repetitions. After sprint training she can go for a run or hike with her family. Over the course of a few weeks, her sprint time will improve and she will cover the same distance in less time. After all endurance sessions Ellie is stretched at home following the stretching routine in *The Healthy Way to Stretch Your Dog* that most matches her primary activity of the day—running, agility or sled pulling.

Intermediate sprint, 30 to 90 seconds run time

To increase intermediate sprinting speed, improving efficiency of both the anaerobic and aerobic metabolic pathways is required. Both metabolic pathways must be used since the first 30 seconds of running utilizes the anaerobic metabolic pathway for energy and then the aerobic metabolic pathway begins to provide energy (Wilmore and Costill, 2005). Since the body must utilize both of these systems, both types of endurance training are required: short sprint training discussed above for the anaerobic pathway; and intermediate distance training for the aerobic pathways. When endurance training for intermediate sprinting distances for activities such as lure coursing, sessions should include short distance sprint training for power off the start line followed by run distances that equal the total distance of a course. The sprinting portion of the program might be achieved by asking the handler to hold the dog at a start line then releasing or luring him toward the handler who is approximately a distance that takes 30 seconds for the dog to cover. For each consecutive run, the value of the reward is increased, ramping up the dog's drive, and therefore his speed. Other types of training are required for optimal run quality in agility, for example, a dog training to compete in agility should undergo strength training for power of the start line and balance training for fast reaction time.

To increase speed for run times over 30 seconds, interval training at total course distance (for example, a lure course) is an option. This type of training should be completed after sprint training when the body has used up the anaerobic energy stores and is primed to begin using the aerobic pathway. Intermediate distance training should consist of asking the dog to run for the total amount of time required in a competition run. For example, if the dog runs a 60 second course and the goal is to run the course in 50 seconds, training should begin with asking the dog to run the distance in 60 seconds. Then, over a period of a few weeks, increase the speed so at the end of the training program the dog is running the same distance in 50 seconds. This can be achieved with ground work on a track or field. For both types of training, the number of repetitions required to meet the training outcome are based on the dog's baseline endurance which will be tested before beginning training.

Long distance endurance, more than 90 seconds

Overloading the body to improve aerobic metabolism for improved endurance for 90 seconds or more requires increasing the body's aerobic efficiency (sled dog racing requires very specific training methods that will not be discussed here). This is achieved by slowly increasing total time exercising over a number of months until the desired time-to-distance ratio is achieved. For example, if the endurance goal is to do an eight-hour hike, the training program might begin in the late winter with two hour hikes three days a week and then working up to a total of eight hours over a period of months. Allowing the body a span of time in which to accommodate to the higher intensity activity helps decrease the probability of sustaining injuries while increasing the quality of endurance for overall improvements in vitality.

From an endurance perspective, running and hiking in the summer can easily translate into skijoring in the winter. Since Ellie (on the right in the next photo) can run at high elevations for at least four hours, she can safely run in the snow for this same period of time taking into consideration the depth of the snow. The deeper the snow, the more energy will be required and the less time Ellie will likely run before fatiguing.

Running during summer builds endurance for skijoring in winter.

Training specificity

The principle of specificity states that endurance training will not improve balance, strength or flexibility. The principle that sprint training will not improve endurance is true, and conversely, distance training will not improve sprint times. For this reason, it is important to determine the endurance training goal before training is initiated. If a dog participates in many different activities, such as an agility dog who day hikes, both kinds of training need to be included in a program. However, if this dog has an important agility trial coming up and needs to have fast run times, it is recommended that distance endurance training be decreased and sprint training increased for the six weeks prior to the event. This time frame will allow the process of cellular adaptation to increase efficiency of the anaerobic metabolic pathway for improved run times.

Progressing an endurance training program

Progressing an endurance training program is different than that for balance and strength training. Whereas cellular adaptation for balance and strength training takes approximately twelve weeks to complete, the cycle of cellular cellular adaptation for endurance training happens during each training session. This is why endurance training can be undertaken three to five times during the week compared to balance and strength training which should occur only twice a week with at least forty eight hours between sessions. Progression for endurance changes frquently keeping the body in the process of cellular adaptation.

To progress a dog through an endurance training program, begin by taking the endurance tests discussed below. Write the test results in an Endurance Training Calendar (see an example on the next page) then fill in the training exercises for the week. At the beginning of each week, retake the endurance test and repeat this process until the dog has met his endurance goal.

Endurance training tests and exercises

To have a clear understanding of which endurance exercises to complete, first determine which type of endurance training your dog needs for their primary activity by reviewing the sidebar below. If your dog participates in activities that use more than one type of endurance training, include both in the conditioning program always starting a session with the shorter distances so the body has used the anaerobic system and is primed to begin using the aerobic system. To capture the times and distances of the endurance test(s), take the Training Program form(s) and write down the times as the endurance test progresses. With each training session, three to five per week, fill in the form to monitor the dog's progress. When the endurance goal is met, continue training at that level or change the goal so running times become even faster or distances longer. If completing endurance training on the same day as other conditioning components complete balance and strength first followed by endurance exercises.

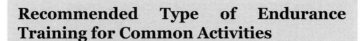

Recommended Type of Endurance Training for Common Activities

- Short distance sprint (<20 seconds): Agility, Dock Diving, Weight Pulling, Flyball

- Intermediate distance sprint (20 – 90 seconds): Lure Coursing, Herding Trials, Obedience

- Long distance running (>90 seconds): Field Work, Hiking, Service Work, Skijoring, Sled racing, Therapy Work, Distance Running

Short & Intermediate Distance Sprint Training Calendar

Endurance Goal
Time: _____
Distance: _____

Endurance Test
Time 1: _____
Time 2: _____
Time 3: _____
Average: _____
Distance: _____

	Session 1	Session 2	Session 3	Session 4	Session 5
Week One	Time 1: ___ Time 2: ___ Time 3: ___ Time 4: ___ Time 5: ___ Average Time:	Time 1: ___ Time 2: ___ Time 3: ___ Time 4: ___ Time 5: ___ Average Time:	Time 1: ___ Time 2: ___ Time 3: ___ Time 4: ___ Time 5: ___ Average Time:	Time 1: ___ Time 2: ___ Time 3: ___ Time 4: ___ Time 5: ___ Average Time:	Time 1: ___ Time 2: ___ Time 3: ___ Time 4: ___ Time 5: ___ Average Time:
Week Two	Time 1: ___ Time 2: ___ Time 3: ___ Time 4: ___ Time 5: ___ Average Time:	Time 1: ___ Time 2: ___ Time 3: ___ Time 4: ___ Time 5: ___ Average Time:	Time 1: ___ Time 2: ___ Time 3: ___ Time 4: ___ Time 5: ___ Average Time:	Time 1: ___ Time 2: ___ Time 3: ___ Time 4: ___ Time 5: ___ Average Time:	Time 1: ___ Time 2: ___ Time 3: ___ Time 4: ___ Time 5: ___ Average Time:
Week Three	Time 1: ___ Time 2: ___ Time 3: ___ Time 4: ___ Time 5: ___ Average Time:	Time 1: ___ Time 2: ___ Time 3: ___ Time 4: ___ Time 5: ___ Average Time:	Time 1: ___ Time 2: ___ Time 3: ___ Time 4: ___ Time 5: ___ Average Time:	Time 1: ___ Time 2: ___ Time 3: ___ Time 4: ___ Time 5: ___ Average Time:	Time 1: ___ Time 2: ___ Time 3: ___ Time 4: ___ Time 5: ___ Average Time:
Week Four	Time 1: ___ Time 2: ___ Time 3: ___ Time 4: ___ Time 5: ___ Average Time:	Time 1: ___ Time 2: ___ Time 3: ___ Time 4: ___ Time 5: ___ Average Time:	Time 1: ___ Time 2: ___ Time 3: ___ Time 4: ___ Time 5: ___ Average Time:	Time 1: ___ Time 2: ___ Time 3: ___ Time 4: ___ Time 5: ___ Average Time:	Time 1: ___ Time 2: ___ Time 3: ___ Time 4: ___ Time 5: ___ Average Time:

Short and Intermediate Distance Sprint Training Program

Long Distance Endurance Training Calendar

		Endurance Goal				Endurance Test		
		Time: _____ Distance: _____				Time: _____ Distance: _____		

	Session 1	Session 2	Session 3	Session 4	Session 5
Week One	Time: ___ Distance: ___	Time: ___ Distance: ___	Time: ___ Distance: ___	Time: ___ Distance: ___	Time: ___ Distance: ___
Week Two	Time: ___ Distance: ___	Time: ___ Distance: ___	Time: ___ Distance: ___	Time: ___ Distance: ___	Time: ___ Distance: ___
Week Three	Time: ___ Distance: ___	Time: ___ Distance: ___	Time: ___ Distance: ___	Time: ___ Distance: ___	Time: ___ Distance: ___
Week Four	Time: ___ Distance: ___	Time: ___ Distance: ___	Time: ___ Distance: ___	Time: ___ Distance: ___	Time: ___ Distance: ___

Long Distance Training Program

Endurance test and program for short distance sprint training

To get a measure of baseline endurance, determine the short sprinting distance required for your dog. Choose an object of high value that the dog will run to such as a favorite treat or toy. In a secure area, place your dog at the start line with a handler. Release the dog with a cue and time the run. Repeat three times. Take the average time as the baseline endurance time. To endurance train, complete these sprints three to five times a week marking down the times during each session. When the endurance goal is met, increase the goal or continue training at that level to maintain endurance gains.

Endurance test and program for intermediate distance sprint training

To get baseline endurance, determine the intermediate sprinting distance required for your dog. Choose an object of high value that the dog will run to. Place your dog at the start line with a handler. Release the dog toward the reward with a cue and time the run. Repeat three times. Take the average time as the baseline endurance time. To endurance train, complete these sprints three to five times a week marking down the times during each session. When the endurance goal is met, increase the goal or continue training at that level to maintain endurance gains.

Endurance test and program for long distance training

To get baseline endurance, choose a secure area or on a treadmill to determine the dog's baseline distance endurance. Over five minutes bring the dog up to the speed required of the activity at a walk, trot or run. Continue at the chosen speed until the dog shows signs of fatigue such as excessive panting or increased spine movement. Note that when a dog is not fatigued he will have good control of his core muscles and his back will not sway appreciably. As he tires, these muscles fatigue and back movement becomes loose. Write down the distance covered and the amount of time the dog exercised. This is the baseline distance endurance time. To endurance train, complete this distance three to five times a week marking down the times during each session. When the endurance goal is met, increase the goal or continue training at that level to maintain endurance gains.

Sled racing requires long distance endurance training.

Knowledge Assessment, True or False
Endurance exercises can be done the same day as strength exercises. True.

There are different types of endurance exercises including sprinting and long distance. True.

Endurance training will increase strength. False.

CHAPTER 6

Activity Specific Cross Training Programs

What separates a cross training program from other conditioning programs is that, by virtue of the four conditioning components and their specific conditioning principles, the program is adaptable throughout the lifetime of the dog allowing him to do his best at a wide range of activities. This flexibility can provide a puppy with age-appropriate exercises, then provide the same dog with a program to support agility training and then modify the program to prepare for summer hiking.

After taking the fitness tests for each component—balance, strength and endurance—you now know your dog's baseline conditioning. If you would like your dog to enjoy better overall health, completing all of the exercises is a great way to optimize all the body systems. If you would like you dog to be physically prepared for the demands of specific activities, recommendations for exercises and the intensity level needed to complete the activities with a new level of vitality are provided here. Each activity specific program comes directly from physical therapy conditioning programs at the *Canine Fitness Zone*. These cross training programs have conditioned top ranked conformation dogs, international agility competitors, and competitive field champions. They have also been used in workshops I have conducted including *Dachshund Back Health, Fitness for Puppies* and *This Old Dog Feels Good*. If a dog participates in an activity that is not included in this chapter, choose a similar activity. If a similar activity cannot be found, contact *Canine Fitness Zone* for a customized conditioning program. All stretching routines can be found in the book or DVD, *The Healthy Way to Stretch Your Dog*.

Activity specific cross training

All conditioning programs should not be the same. Different activities place varied levels and types of stress on the body. Well designed conditioning programs should meet the demands of specific activities. This is achieved by including exercises from all four conditioning components that meet the physical requirements of particular activity specific competitions or hobbies. These diverse combinations of exercises, when employed correctly, meld together to produce a more successful fitness plan for each dog.

Cross training recommendations are discussed below for a variety of activities in alphabetical order.

Agility

Agility is a full-body, multi-planar, high energy activity that requires an exceptional level of conditioning. All agility cross training programs should begin with balance, focusing on core stabilization and whole body awareness exercises, which are to be completed with impeccable posture and control. These exercises build a strong core from which all movement emanates. In an agility cross training program, both front and rear limb strengthening exercises should be included. The front limb exercises bolster the muscles and nerves that generate novel movement patterns such as front limb abduction (moving the limb away from the body) in the weave poles that can place repetitive stresses on the medial portion of the shoulder joint. Rear limb strengthening exercises can increase muscular support of the hips and stifle while increasing power off the start line. Short distance sprint training prepares the dog for multiple runs with fatigue resistance. The Agility Stretching Routine from *The Healthy Way to Stretch Your Dog*, when completed after exercises and trials, returns the muscles to their natural length, storing elasticity for the next bout of exercises. A well balanced agility cross training program will optimize conditioning and it may also increase speed for faster runs while solidifying movement quality for fewer run errors. If a dog is completing in agility recreationally, working up to Level Three balance and strength exercises should be the goal. If a dog is highly competitive, reaching for Level Four and beyond is highly recommended.

Conformation

For purebred dogs, a cross training program can enhance natural conformation in the ring. Balance exercises, particularly core stabilization exercises, improve a dog's top-line. Strength of the rear limb improves the power of drive. Breed-specific endurance exercises brings out vitality in the ring and prevents dogs from showing well early in the competition and tiring as the weekend wears on. The Conformation Stretching Routine from *The Healthy Way to Stretch Your Dog*, when completed after exercise or a day of competition, increases muscle length, a primary component in balanced reach and drive. In the proper combination, a cross training program can help reveal a dog's natural "it-factor" in the ring while supporting their out-of-ring activities. For conformation dogs, working up to Level Two core stabilization and front and rear limb strength exercises build well balanced bodies that bring out a dog's natural vitality in the ring.

Dachshund Back Health

This program is designed as foundation conditioning for all Dachshunds and should be started with the Puppy Program. When mature, dogs should be transitioned to this program. By strengthening the core stabilizing muscles, a layer of muscular support is provided to the back. Whole body awareness increases the quality of movement, and front and rear limb strengthening exercises keep the entire body strong to help offset the external forces encountered in daily living. If a Dachshund participates in other activities such as agility, the agility cross training program should be utilized. The recommended exercise intensity for balance and strength is at least Level Two. Endurance exercises should be short or intermediate sprints. The stretching program should include activity specific stretching.

Dock diving

Although water appears to be yielding, it actually has enough density to cause injury to the hips, back and tail if the back and abdominal muscles are not powerful enough to withstand the force of hitting the water. As the dog jumps from the dock, his front limbs reach forward following his eyes as his back limbs are fully extended from the dock for take-off. If the dog has not learned how to pull their back feet forward after the take-off, contracting his core and protecting himself from back extension injuries, he may hit the water in this fully extended position. Including balance, particularly core stabilization, rear limb strengthening exercises, sprinting endurance exercises, and the Dock Diving Stretching Routine from *The Healthy Way to Stretch Your Dog* will help prepare the dog for highly competitive jumps while decreasing the probability of sustaining injuries. Working up to Level Four core stabilization and rear limb strength exercises is highly recommended (look at photos on pages 21 and 22 to see how core stabilization carries over into jumping ability).

Fieldwork

Field work demands incredible endurance on uneven terrain and pristine full body control. Having the energy required to move over large distances can be achieved with distance endurance exercises. Helping the body automatically manage uneven terrain while the dog is working can be done with front and rear limb strengthening exercises, particularly those exercises that strengthen and lengthen the Biceps muscle (to decrease the probability of biceps tendonitis) and the hamstring muscle group (to support the cranial cruciate ligament). Stretching should always be completed after conditioning exercises and after field work to prevent muscular imbalances. The stretching Field Work Routine can be found in *The Healthy Way to Stretch Your Dog*. Working up to Level Three core stabilization, whole body awareness and front limb (particularly push-ups) and rear limb strengthening is recommended.

Flyball

This activity requires quick bursts of energy plus excellent eccentric (lengthening) control of the carpal (wrist) and tarsal (ankle) muscles to prevent muscle strain injuries. Conditioning to optimize Flyball should include working up to Level Four balance exercises—both core stabilization and whole body awareness, front (especially push-ups) and rear limb strengthening, and sprint endurance training. All bouts of training and conditioning should include the Flyball stretching routine in *The Healthy Way to Stretch Your Dog*.

Herding

Herding requires fast, tight, unpredictable movements on uneven terrain. Similar to agility, the level of conditioning required to successfully herd without sustaining injuries is very high. Because of the inherent drive of the most common herding breeds, many injuries may go unseen as the dog drives through the injury. Adding a conditioning program to a herding dog's life as early as possible will help to build a foundation of balance, strength, endurance, and flexibility that will inspire safe high quality trials. All herding programs should include balance exercises—core stabilization and whole body awareness. Strengthening exercises should include front limb exercises to support navigation on uneven terrain and rear limb exercises to support rear limb joints while allowing for good acceleration and deceleration in the field. Both of these exercise components should be worked up to Level Four. Endurance exercises should match the activity requirements of the highest intensity trial. Stretching should occur after exercises or trials and recommendations can be found in *The Healthy Way to Stretch Your Dog*.

Hiking

Hiking requires uphill walking, trotting or running on uneven terrain for extended periods of time—then returning downhill when the muscles are fatigued. Dogs often outpace their owners during a hike, moving distances three to four times the actual trail distance. Because they are hiking longer distances, they may fatigue before the hike downhill is initiated. It is during the portion of the hike coming down in elevation when the muscles are contracting eccentrically (lengthening to control the movement) that the dog is most at risk for injuries (as are we). Conditioning them so they are prepared to enjoy mountain hikes with a lower risk of injury, their cross training program should include balance exercises (working up to Level Three), rear and front limb strengthening exercises (working up to

Level Three), and endurance training to build the heart and lungs. Of great importance is allowing the body time to build up to a hiking level of conditioning. At least three months of conditioning is required to prepare a couch dog for high mountain summer hiking.

Old dogs

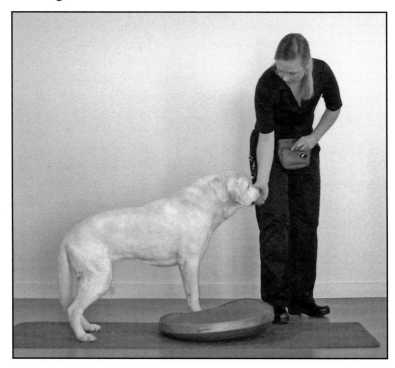

To maintain function for getting up off the floor, up and down steps, in and out of the car and to have enough energy to participate in daily family activities, old dogs should maintain Level Two balance and strength exercises. As dogs age, arthritis or other degenerative processes may negate them from completing exercises at levels higher than this. If your dog has been on a cross training program of some type for his entire life and has been cleared by both a veterinarian and a CCRT, then completing exercises above Level Two may be appropriate. For a dog who has never been on a cross training program, having a CCRT design a program specifically for your dog is highly recommended to prevent exacerbating underlying musculoskeletal or neurological conditions, particularly for endurance exercises which need to match the dog's physical condition. The stretching routine should be the old dog routine in *The Healthy Way to Stretch Your Dog*.

Puppies

Salem is ten months old. She is being transitioned to Level Two whole body awareness exercises after completing Level One at six months of age.

Working to promote overall health should begin when dogs are still puppies. At this early stage in life, easy exercises inspire the nervous system to build strong neural networks that will carry-over in all activities when a dog is mature. Just as importantly, avoiding exercises that are too difficult such as leash running, long hikes and competition performance events will help decrease the probability of unseen micro-injuries to muscles, ligaments and bones that may silently fester until a dog is mature. Good puppy exercises include Level One balance and strength exercises. Until they begin to reach maturity, puppies should not complete structured endurance training or stretching. The repetitive action of endurance training can put stresses on growing supportive tissues such as tendons and ligaments. Puppies are naturally flexible; it is too easy to over-stretch their muscles predisposing them to muscle strains.

Running

Like human runners, the repetitive action of running can cause tightness in particular muscle groups that lead to muscular imbalances in strength that predispose a dog to muscle strains. A cross training program that includes balance (working up to Level Two), in particular core stabilization exercises, strengthening exercises (working up to Level Two), and flexibility exercises as well as endurance training will help prevent muscular imbalances. Please see the Running Stretching Routine in *The Healthy Way to Stretch Your Dog*.

Search and Rescue

These dogs save lives; they deserve the highest quality conditioning programs. To help prevent body breakdown during SAR, it is highly recommended that these dogs train at elite levels, at least Level Four balance and strength exercises. It is also recommended that they train both short distance sprint training and long distance endurance training as the metabolic pathways that support both of these systems are required to complete their work. After all bouts of exercise, they should enjoy the SAR Stretching Routine found in *The Healthy Way to Stretch Your Dog*.

Service work

Service dogs are an organic extension of the person they work with. A conditioning program that builds overall health will help these dogs have the stamina required to complete their jobs joyfully. A global conditioning program should include balance exercises (working up to Level Two), strength exercises (working up to Level Two), endurance exercises and a stretching routine. If the physical limitations of the human prevent them from completing the exercises with the dog, it is highly recommended a friend, neighbor or volunteer complete the program. It takes extraordinary effort to train these dogs to do this work. The effort required to keep them in top condition is well worth the time and energy required as it may help decrease the risk of physical injuries associated with work as well as providing an outlet for learning the skills necessary for service dog work.

Sled Pulling

Much research has been completed on endurance conditioning for long distance sled pulling. What has not been included in these programs are the other three conditioning components, balance, strength and flexibility. For sled pulling, balance work can strengthen the core stabilizing muscles providing a strong anchor for repetitive limb movement. Strengthening of the front and rear limbs can create more balanced movement. Flexibility can prevent repetitive overuse injuries of muscles (see the Sled Pulling Routine in *The Healthy Way to Stretch Your Dog*). Understanding that it can be difficult to condition an entire team of dogs one at a time, *Canine Fitness Zone* has created team cross training protocols that include the three additional conditioning components. Please contact CFZ individually for more information (www.caninefitnesszone.com). For individual work-outs, focus on Level Three core stabilization, whole body awareness, and front and rear limb strengthening to improve overall conditioning.

Therapy work

Therapy dogs have to demonstrate very good impulse control including a high level of body awareness to work with many different types of individuals in the community. A well designed cross training program can increase the fitness level of these dogs so they complete their jobs with a higher level of vitality and body awareness. The exercises learned in the conditioning program can be utilized out in the community to teach individuals the importance of fitness. Exercises for therapy dogs should include balance exercises (working up to Level Two), front and rear limb strengthening exercises (Level Two), short to intermediate distance endurance exercises and the whole-body stretching routine in *The Healthy Way to Stretch Your Dog*.

Weight pulling

Power stored in the hip and chest muscles creates the force required to pull loads that far exceed a dog's body weight. To help these muscles have an anchor for movement, balance exercises including core stabilization are recommended. The purpose of strengthening exercises is to prevent muscular imbalances that can lead to injuries. For example, strength of the Gluteal muscle group is required for weight pulling. Over time this can cause excessive tightness in this muscle group predisposing the muscle on the opposite side of the leg, the Iliopsoas muscle, to strain injuries. Strength training can maintain muscle balance for higher quality, injury-free pulls. Endurance exercise should include short distance sprint training as this will help the muscles store large amounts of energy for very short periods of time. A conditioning program should work these dogs up to Level Four balance and strength and higher.

The Cross Training Team

Taking photos for a book is a fun challenge. Taking photos for a book with dogs requires additional humor and patience. Getting amazing shots of dogs doing exercises in a room full of cords and lights and a camera snapping requires something special. These teams have what it takes; they make it look easy. By virtue of their relationships with their dogs, their commitment to conditioning, and their training consistency, the photo shoots were simple and fun. These teams are shining examples of the power of the human-animal bond and how it's strengthened when the dogs have a voice and a choice in everything they do.

In order of appearance:

Human: Kassy Hill

Dog: CH Doxikota Strauss's Dirty Denim TD NA NAJ CGC, aka "Strauss"

Age: 4 1/2

Favorite Activity: Chasing rabbits and agility

Favorite Exercise: Anything with the peanut

Dog: Sunbeam Met Starline at Big Ben, aka "Benny"

Age: 21 months

Favorite Activity: Running!

Favorite Exercise: Back feet on the box

Human: Sarah Stremming, CPDT-KA

Dog: Whistlestop's Bee Charmer, AX,, AXJ,, OF, aka "Idgie"

Age: 3

Favorite Activity: Agility

Favorite exercise: Long distance endurance hiking in the mountains

Humans: Chris and Helen Homquist-Johnson

Dog: Copper Rose Holmquist-Johnson, NA, NAJ

Age: 4

Favorite Activity: Agility, skateboarding

Favorite Exercise: Doggie sun salutation (core stability Level three)

Dog: Lady Aspen Holmquist-Johnson

Age: 13

Favorite Activity: Walks around the neighborhood, digging in the sandbox

Favorite Exercise: Front feet on box

Human: Ashley Foster, CPDT-KA

Dog: Ch. Imagemaker's Break The Ice, aka "Breaker"

Age: 4

Favorite Activity: Conformation and learning new stuff!

Favorite Exercise: Wobble board with all fours!

Human: Laura Southworth

Dog: Ellie Mae, aka "Ellie"

Age: 5 years

Favorite Activity: Agility and long hikes treasure hunting in the woods

Favorite Exercise: Doggie sun salutations and any exercise with independent back feet

Human: Ashley Eike

Dog: McVan's Something Wicked, aka "Salem"

Age: 10 months

Favorite Activity: Baby dog agility

Favorite Exercise: Feet on the disc!

Balance Training Calendar

Frequency: Twice a week
Intensity: Core, 5 reps; WBA, 10 reps
Duration: Twelve weeks

Goal:

Exercise	Current Level				1	2	3	4	5	6	7	8	9	10	11	12	re-test
Core Stability	1	2	3	4													
Whole Body Awareness	1	2	3	4													

Strength Training Calendar

Frequency: Twice a week

Intensity: Ten controlled repetitions

Duration: Twelve weeks/eight weeks

Goal:

	Exercise	Current Level				1	2	3	4	5	6	7	8	9	10	11	12	re-test
Front Limb	Side-stepping	1	2	3	4													
	Push-ups	1	2	3	4													
Rear Limb	Side-stepping	1	2	3	4													
	Sit-to-stand	1	2	3	4													

BIBLIOGRAPHY

Barroso, R., Tricoli, V., Gil, S., Ugrinowitsch, C., and H. Roschel. "Maximal strength, number of repetitions, and total volume are differently affected by static-, ballistic-, and PNF- stretching." *J Strength Cond Res*. 2011 Nov 5. Retrieved Jan 2012 via PubMed.

Coffey, V.G. and J.A. Hawley. "The molecular bases of training adaptation." *Sports Med*. 37.9 (2007):737-63.

Duchateau, J., and R.M. Enoka. "Human motor unit recordings: origins and insight into the integrated motor system." *Brain Res*. 1490 (29 Aug 2011):42-61. Epub 2011 Jun 13

Foerder Preston, Mallory Galloway, Tony Barthel, Donald E. Moore III, and Diana Reiss. "Insightful problem solving in an Asian elephant." *PLoS One*. 6.8.e23251 (2011). Retrieved 18 Aug 2011 via Epub: 10.1371/journal.pone.0023251

Folland, J.P., and A.G Williams. "The adaptations to strength training: morphological and neurological contributions to increased strength." *Sports Med*. 37.2 (2007):145-68.

Foster, Sasha and Ashley. *The Healthy Way to Stretch Your Dog. A Physical Therapy Approach*. Dogwise Publishing, 2009.

Gabriel, D.A., Kamen, G.,and G. Frost "Neural adaptations to resistive exercise: mechanisms and recommendations for training practices." *Sports Med*. 36.2 (2006):133-49.

Garrett, Susan. *Shaping Success. The Education of an Unlikely Champion*. Clean Run Press, 2005.

Ghez, Claude. "Muscles: Effectors of the Motor Systems." *Principles of Neural Science, 3rd ed*. Eric R. Kandel, James H. Schwarz and Thomas M. Jessell. Connecticut, Appleton and Lange, 1991. 548-63.

Hawley JA, LM Burke, SM Phillips and LL Spriett. "Nutritional modulation of training-induced skeletal muscle adaptations." *J Appl Physiol.* 110.3 (Mar 2011):834-45. Epub 2010 Oct 28.

Hebert, JJ, SL Koppenhaver, JS Magel, JM Fritz. "The relationship of transversus abdominis and lumbar multifidus activation and prognostic factors for clinical success with a stabilization exercise program: a cross-sectional study." *Arch Phys Med Rehabil.* 91.1 (Jan 2010): 78-85.

Jaeger, Gayle, and Sherman O. Canapp. "Carpal and Tarsal Injuries." *Clean Run.* 14.5 (May 2008): 74-6

Kandel, Eric. "Perception of Motion, Depth and Form." *Principles of Neural Science, 3rd ed.* Eric R. Kandel, James H. Schwarz and Thomas M. Jessell. Connecticut, Appleton and Lange, 1991. 440-66.

Kostrubiec V, R Soppelso, JM Albaret, and PG Zanone. "Facilitation of nonpreferred coordination patterns during the transition from discrete to continuous movements." *Motor Control.* 15.4 (Oct 2011):456-80.

Kubukeli, ZN, TD Noakes, and SC Dennis. "Training techniques to improve endurance exercise performances." *Sports Med.* 32.8 (2002):489-509.

S G Lisberger, E J Morris, and L Tychsen. "Visual Motor Processing and Sensory-Motor Integration for Smooth Pursuit Eye Movements." *Annual Review of Neuroscience.* Vol. 10 (March 1987): 97-129

Martin, John H. and Thomas M. Jessell. "Modality Coding in the Somatic Sensory System." *Principles of Neural Science, 3rd ed.* Eric R. Kandel, James H. Schwarz and Thomas M. Jessell. Appleton and Lange, 1991. 341-52.

Mujika I., and S. Padilla. "Detraining: loss of training-induced physiological and performance adaptations. Part I: short term insufficient training stimulus." *Sports Med.* 30.2 (Aug 2000):79-87.

Mujika I., and S. Padilla. "Detraining: loss of training-induced physiological and performance adaptations. Part II: short term insufficient training stimulus." *Sports Med.* 30.3 (Sep 2000):145-54.

Muthukrishnan, R., S.D. Shenoy, S.S. Jaspal, S. Nellikunja, and S. Fernandes. "The differential effects of core stabilization exercise regime and conventional physiotherapy regime on postural control parameters during perturbation in patients with movement and control impairment chronic low back pain." *Sports Med Arthrosc Rehabil Ther Technol.* (31 May 2010): 2:13. Retrieved 1 Jan 2012 from http://www.ncbi.nlm.nih.gov/pubmed/20103400.

Oya, T., Riek, S., and A.G. Cresswell. "Recruitment and rate coding organisation for soleus motor units across entire range of voluntary isometric plantar flexions." *J Physiol.* 587.19 (1 Oct 2009):4737-48. Epub 2009 Aug 24.

Shalit, U., Zinger, N., Joshua, M., and Y. Prut. "Descending Systems Translate Transient Cortical Commands into a Sustained Muscle Activation Signal." *Cereb Cortex.* 30 Sep 2011. [Epub ahead of print]

Simon, D.A. and Bjork, R.A. "Metacognition in motor learning." *Journal of Experimental Psychology,* 27.4 (July 2001): 907-12.

Tsang, K.K., and A.A. DiPasquale. "Improving the Q:H strength ratio in women using plyometric exercises." *J Strength Cond Res.* 25.10 (Oct 2011):2740-5.

Human research has shown that lactic acid build-up and slower sprint times are directly correlated. (Twist, C., and R. Eston. "The effects of exercise-induced muscle damage on maximal intensity intermittent exercise performance." *Eur J Appl Physiol.* 94.5-6 (Aug 2005):652-8. Epub May 11 2005.)

Warraich Z, and JA Kleim. "Neural plasticity: the biological substrate for neurorehabilitation." *PM&R.* 2.12.2 (Dec 2010):S208-19.

Wilmore, Jack, and David Costill. *Physiology of Sport and Exercise: 3rd edition.* Human Kinetics Publishing, 2005.

ABOUT THE AUTHOR

Sasha A. Foster has her Master's Degree in Physical Therapy from Arcadia University in Glenside, Pennsylvania and is certified canine rehabilitation therapist through Canine Rehab Institute in Wellington, Florida. She is the co-founder of Canine Fitness Zone, Inc. (CFZ), providing research-based physical therapy and sports rehabilitation services at four Colorado Front Range clinics including Colorado State University Veterinary Teaching Hospital in Fort Collins, Colorado. At CFZ, Sasha also hosts annual continuing education programs for dog owners and certified canine rehabilitation therapists including the CFZ 4-Tiered Athletic Conditioning Program, Nutrition for Performance, and Injury Identification. She is a faculty member of Canine Rehab Institute teaching Therapist Module and Pain Management. Her first co-authored book, *The Healthy Way to Stretch Your Dog, A Physical Therapy Approach*, won the 2009 Maxwell Award for Best Health & Care Book; it is now available as a DVD. She can be contacted at sasha@caninefitnesszone.com.

INDEX

A

activity specific cross training programs, 105–114

adenosine triphosphate (ATP), 91, 94, 96

aerobic metabolism, 92, 95, 97

age factors, 92, 110–111

aggravation, 17

agility programs, 106–107

anaerobic metabolism, 91, 94, 97

arthritis, 110

ATP (adenosine triphosphate), 91, 94, 97

awareness of whole body. *See* whole body awareness

B

balance
building principles, 19–23
exercises for, 32–39
overview, 7–8
tests for, 23–31
training specificity and, 10

Balance Training Calendar, 24, 122

Barroso, R., 7

behaviors, foundational, 15–17

Bjork, R.A., 12

blood sugar, 92, 94, 96

breed differences, 10, 93, 107

C

Canine Fitness Zone, 1–2, 26, 55, 60, 65, 105–106, 113

carbohydrates, 92

cellular adaption
balance tests and, 23
during endurance training, 94–99
overview, 9
strength tests and, 51
for strength training, 63–66

Coffey, V.G., 9

cognitive learning, 12

components of conditioning, 6–7

conditioning components and principles, 6–11

conformation, 107

core stability
building balance and, 20–21
endurance training and, 92
exercises for, 32–39
tests for, 23–31

Costill, David, 8, 64, 94, 97

cross training program teams, 115–121

D

dachshund back health, 107

Dachshund Back Health workshops, 105

delayed-onset-muscle-soreness (DOMS), 33, 40, 64–65

DiPasquale, A.A., 66

disuse of training, 11

dock diving, 108

DOMS (delayed-onset-muscle-soreness), 33, 40, 64–65

Duchateau, J., 51

E

encoding of nervous system, 13–14

L

lactic acid, 64–65, 94, 96
learning, motor, 12–17
limb reaction time, 22–23
Lisberger, S.G., 13
long distance endurance, 98, 102–103
Long Distance Endurance Training Calendar, 102

M

Martin, John H., 21
maximizing motor unit recruitment, 51, 66
metabolic pathways, 91–97
motor learning, 12–17
motor unit
  activation of, 63–66
  definition, 51
Mujika, I., 11
muscles
  in activity specific cross training, 106–114
  breed differences and, 10
  building balance and, 19–21, 23–24, 33–35
  building endurance and, 91–92, 94–95
  building strength and, 50–52, 64–68, 72
  cellular adaption, 9
  delayed-onset-muscle-soreness (DOMS), 33, 40, 64–65
  neural encoding and, 13–14
  stretching, 7

N

natural conformation, 38

neural encoding, 13–17
neural plasticity, definition, 12
nutrition for endurance training, 92

O

older dogs, 110–111
overload principle
  balance tests and, 23
  for endurance training, 95–98
  overview, 8–9

P

Padilla, S., 11
paw targeting, 15–16
plateau of strength training, 63–66
postural stabilizing muscles, 20–21
pre-program assessment tests. See tests, pre-program
principles of conditioning, 8–11
progression of program, overview, 10
proprioceptive fibers, 20–21, 33
puppies, 111

R

running, 112

S

safety, 3–4
search and rescue, 112
sensory input from body, 19–20
service work, 112
Shalit, U., 51
shaping by successive approximation, 14

Also available from Dogwise Publishing

Go to www.dogwise.com for more books and ebooks.

The Healthy Way to Stretch Your Dog
A Physical Therapy Approach
Sasha Foster, MSPT, CCRT and Ashley Foster, CPDT-KA

You have probably heard that humans need to stretch for good health. So do dogs. Now you can learn how to safely and effectively stretch your dog to prevent injuries, maintain joint integrity, and improve your dog's fitness, whether he is an elite canine athlete or a lap dog.

The Healthy Way to Stretch Your Dog
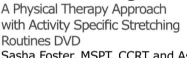
A Physical Therapy Approach with Activity Specific Stretching Routines DVD
Sasha Foster, MSPT, CCRT and Ashley Foster, CPDT-KA

This DVD demonstrates how to safely and effectively stretch each major muscle group. Teaches correct hand placement for joint stabilization and how to maintain good form. Stretching routines are presented for both large and small dogs, older dogs, and those that are involved in a variety of dog sports.

Canine Massage, 2nd Ed.
A Complete Reference Manual
Jean-Pierre Hourdebaigt, L.M.T.

Bring the well-known benefits of massage to your own dog or become a canine massage specialist. Over 100 illustrations and 100 photos, detailed examinations of muscular stress points, diagnoses, and treatments.

Canine Massage
In 3 Easy Steps DVD
Natalie Lenton

Whether you are a complete novice, or have experience with massage, this DVD is a must for every dog owner who wants to improve or maintain their dog's quality of life, mobility and comfort level. Within one hour, this DVD will give you all the knowledge you need to massage your dog like a professional.

Dogwise.com your source for quality books, ebooks, DVDs, training tools and treats.

We've been selling to the dog fancier for more than 25 years and we carefully screen our products for quality information, safety, durability and FUN! You'll find something for every level of dog enthusiast on our website www.dogwise.com or drop by our store in Wenatchee, Washington.